MW00615811

the FLOWER-INFUSED COCKTAIL

the FLOWER-INFUSED COCKTAIL

Flowers, with a *Twist*

ALYSON BROWN
founder of Wild Folk Flower Apothecary

folk
PUBLISHING

First published in the United States in 2021
by Folk Publishing.
Printed and bound in China.

10 9 8 7 6 5 4 3 2 1

ISBN: 978-1-7366989-0-7 (hardcover)
ISBN: 978-1-7366989-1-4 (ebook)

Photography and book design by Alyson Brown
Edited by Camille Lazelle de Zapata
Glass illustrations by Off The Hook Studio

The material contained in this book is presented only for informational and artistic purposes. If you use flowers or plants for any of the recipes included in this book, the author and publisher suggest you only use items from reputable vendors, farmers markets, or grocery stores. If you choose to use flowers or plants you may have found in the wild, you are doing so at your own risk. Foraging wild ingredients requires expert knowledge and identification. The author accepts no responsibility or liability for any error, omission, or misrepresentation expressed or implied, contained herein or for any accidents, harmful reactions, or any other specific reactions, injuries, loss, legal consequences, or incidental damages suffered or incurred by any reader of this book. This content is accurate and true to the best of the author's knowledge and is not meant to substitute for formal and individualized advice from a qualified professional.

To those who celebrate a
flower-infused lifestyle and
appreciate flowers beyond
their beauty — cheers!

Imagine you're sitting at a bar, looking at the cocktail menu. Elderflower is an ingredient in a delightful sounding drink, but you've never heard of elderflower and you aren't quite sure how it tastes. Or maybe you have tasted elderflowers and know they're quite delicious, but you don't know a thing about their history. What if I told you that elderflowers were rich with folklore, superstition, and medicinal powers — altogether perhaps more than any other plant? Would that make you want to taste them, experience them, and know even more?

I founded Wild Folk Flower Apothecary out of a desire to celebrate a flower-infused lifestyle. I knew I was meant to work with flowers and it was a way to share my love of flowers with the world. I felt a deep connection to them, and I wanted to know more. Once I slowed down and paid attention to the way different flowers made me feel, I wanted to know about their symbolism, folklore, and use throughout history. I wanted to know how that was connected to me and how I could infuse different flowers into the things I used around me. That meant everything from the flowers I brought home from the flower shop to the tea that I drank, baths I took, skincare I used, food I ate, and of course... the cocktails that I made.

Perhaps you, too, have a love of flowers and, like me, you enjoy crafting cocktails. And maybe you're wanting to know a little more about the flowers around you. I wrote this book as a guide for further understanding of the range of edible flowers, with little notes from their history and folklore and information about how to use them in a cocktail. Inside you will find many recipes for crafting unique drinks from your homemade edible flower pantry. Sometimes flowers are used as an integral ingredient in the cocktail and other times their beauty simply garnishes the drink.

I hope this book gives you inspiration to celebrate flowers beyond the vase and that you enjoy the flower-infused recipes I've dreamt up. Crafting my own flower-infused pantry is so satisfying, and I thoroughly enjoy the process of making my own ingredients whenever possible. However, if you didn't plan the time to make your own, or if perhaps the flowers called for are just out of season, there are many wonderful substitutes out there.

Cheers to a flower-infused lifestyle!

3 STARS
ESPOLÒN
BULLEIT 95 RYE

Building Your Bar

Whether you're just getting started with crafting your own cocktails at home or you're a seasoned bartender, building your bar can be fulfilling but overwhelming. I recommend starting with a few of your favorite base spirits, classic bitters, sturdy glassware, bar tools, and an array of edible flowers. In the next few pages, I'll go over different types of glassware and tools, why they deserve a place at your home bar, and knowledge on edible flower sourcing and safety.

Glassware

Cocktails are served in different glasses, depending on the drink you order. This is a guide of the most popular cocktail glasses. You definitely don't need to go out and purchase every single glass listed here, especially if you're just building your bar. Stick with a classic coupe, collins, and rocks glass as they'll cover most needs. The icon on each cocktail page will let you know which glass should be used.

COLLINS

A tall, skinny glass perfect for serving a fizz or "and" drinks like vodka and tonic.

OLD FASHIONED

Used for shaken drinks served chilled or stirred drinks served over a single large ice cube.

NICK & NORA

Stirred or shaken, spirit-forward drinks. Served without ice.

SNIFTER

Best for serving stirred, spirit-forward drinks. Think nightcaps. Can also be used to serve hot toddies.

MARGARITA

Perfect for serving your favorite margarita blended with ice, rather than on the rocks.

WINE GLASS

Used to serve spritzes or cocktails in which wine is an ingredient.

IRISH COFFEE

A clear, heat-proof glass meant to show off the layers in Irish coffee. Often used for warm drinks or a classic Irish coffee.

ROCKS

For drinks literally served on the rocks, AKA ice. Sometimes served with a straw for easy drinking.

COUPE

Used for serving shaken or stirred cocktails without ice. Popular among the craft-cocktail movement but was originally developed for serving champagne.

MARTINI

For drinks that are served "up." The large surface area, highlights the aromatic elements of the drink

SLING

A tall, footed glass, narrower at the bottom and wider at the top. Used for serving long or tall drinks with ice.

POCO GRANDE

Meant for mixed drinks or punch-style cocktails. Similar to a hurricane glass, but smaller in size.

GOBLET

A multi-purpose glass with thicker walls to provide insulation. Great for serving frozen or slushy drinks.

Home Bar Tools

There are a few must-haves every home mixologist should keep in their cabinet. These are the essentials I recommend and reference throughout the book that will make your cocktail building even simpler.

SHAKER

The shaker comes in two different styles: the cobbler and the Boston. The cobbler is a three-piece shaker with built-in strainer, perfect for the home bar. The Boston shaker consists of two metal tins and can hold more volume — making it more preferable in a bar setting.

STRAINER

There are three primary types of cocktails strainers: the Hawthorne strainer, the Julep strainer, and the fine-mesh strainer. The Hawthorne strainer is for straining a cocktail when using a shaker tin. Additionally, the spring can be removed and doubles as a tool to aid in whipping egg whites. The Julep strainer works best when paired with a mixing glass, and the fine-mesh strainer works overtime when you need a little extra straining.

CITRUS JUICER & PEELER

Fresh juice is always best, so invest in a sturdy, handheld citrus juicer. A peeler is for a citrus peel garnish.

ICE MOLDS

There are many types of ice molds available, but I recommend starting with a large square mold, a small square mold, and a sphere mold.

JIGGER

The jigger is what you'll use to measure ingredients for your cocktail. Different sizes are available for measuring spirits and ingredients. Look for one that measures 1 oz and 2 oz, with markings on the inside for smaller volumes.

MIXING GLASS

To shake or to stir? As a rule, cocktails that contain only alcoholic ingredients should always be stirred. In this case, you need a mixing glass to build the drink.

BAR SPOON

A bar spoon is a long-handled spoon used for stirring and layering drinks. It also holds about 5 mL (1 tsp) of liquid and is used to measure smaller amounts of ingredients.

MUDDLER

Usually wooden with a large and rounded end, the muddler is used to mash ingredients like herbs and fruits.

BOTTLES & JARS

These are for storing infusions, simple syrups and liqueurs. Simple glass jars with a ring lid work great, as well as clean, empty liquor bottles.

Edible Flower Awareness

In my humble opinion, edible flowers are the most magnificent addition to a cocktail. Not only do they add beauty by gracing the rim as a garnish, but they come in an array of complex and delicious flavors. In this book, I'll be exploring not only the familiar ones but also ones that are more unique and less known. With anything edible, there are a few very important things to note:

SOURCING EDIBLE FLOWERS

Often times you can find edible flowers at local farmers markets or specialty grocery stores near the herbs. There are many trusted online sites for flowers as well. You can find a list of my favorites in the resources section of the book on page 153. Be sure never to eat flowers that have been grown as display flowers, as sometimes they have been treated with pesticides and are not considered food grade.

GROW YOUR OWN

Growing your own edible flowers can be very rewarding. They're the perfect addition to your cocktails and can be added to a variety of meals for a flavorful pop of color. Plus, there are many different varieties available that you can grow from seed that you won't find in a grocery store.

PICKING, STORING, AND FORAGING

When picking flowers from your garden, it's best to harvest them first thing in the morning as they're just opening up. Be sure to dust for insects and wash them throughly before using or storing. Flowers are always better when fresh, but the can be kept in the refrigerator in an airtight container for a few days.

If you're foraging for flowers, be 100% sure that you know what you're picking. Many plants have harmful or even deadly lookalikes. It's a good rule of thumb to never forage from the roadside, as there could be toxic runoff from the roads. Never take more than you need. Pick with intention and leave some behind. For example, when picking wild roses, only take a few of the petals from each flower, leaving some behind to attract pollinators.

SAFETY

Safety is the MOST important thing to note when eating something new and out of the ordinary. Do your research. Eat in moderation. Be aware of allergens. I have listed many edible flowers in this book, and in fact, there are many more! However it is extremely important to note that there are some flowers with known contradictions and some that can make you very, very sick if ingested.

Base Spirit Infusions

Infusing base spirits can add unique flavors to your cocktails, and it's quite simple to do. The base spirits are the hard liquors that make up the foundation of the majority of cocktails and liqueurs: brandy, gin, rum, tequila, vodka, and whisk(e)y. Each has distinct flavor that contribute its own unique character to a drink. While the base spirits are great on their own, infusing them with fruits, flowers, herbs, or spices can add a twist to any cocktail. In this chapter you'll find recipes for infusing your own or pre-infused base spirits that I love.

Artichoke

Cynara cardunculus var. scolymus

You're probably thinking I've started this book out on a crazy note. Artichoke, a flower? Yes, indeed! The same artichoke that we know from the produce department is actually a thistle in the same family as the sunflower. Each layer that we pull back and dip into butter is a flower petal on a bud that has yet to bloom.

The globe artichoke we eat today was cultivated from the wild cardoon, a much pricklier flowering plant. A Greek philosopher and naturalist, Theophrastus, first wrote about them growing wild in Italy and Sicily during the 4th-century BCE, yet it wasn't until much later that the artichoke was cultivated and earned a spot in the garden. If left on the plant rather than harvested as food, the artichoke develops a dazzling and spiky purple flower.

Over history, the artichoke has become a symbol of desire. It was considered to be a powerful aphrodisiac and at one point were even forbidden to be eaten. It has since been viewed as a delicacy, favored by the rich. Just be sure to remove the fibrous inside, AKA the "choke," before diving into the heart.

LATE-NIGHT CAROUSEL

makes 1 drink

Have you ever noticed after taking a bite of an artichoke, everything you taste after becomes slightly sweeter? That's because artichokes contain a natural acid that stimulates your sweet-perceiving taste buds. Late-Night Carousel takes advantage of this, making for a little less-bitter riff on the Negroni.

ARTICHOKE-INFUSED VERMOUTH

Add 1 small freshly sliced artichoke heart to a jar and cover with vermouth. Infuse for 1 day and strain. Use within 1 week.

1 oz gin
1 oz artichoke-infused dry vermouth
*1 oz Cynar**
3 dashes of grapefruit bitters
5 drops of Lambrusco vinegar

Stir gin, artichoke-infused vermouth, and Cynar together in a mixing glass with ice until chilled. Strain into a chilled glass over a large cube and dash with bitters and vinegar. Garnish with a grapefruit peel.

**Cynar is a bittersweet amaro flavored by artichokes, herbs, barks, and roots; best enjoyed as an apéritif.*

Begonia

Begonia spp.

Begonias are some of the most popular house plants in the world. There are more than 1,200 species and hybrids including miniatures standing 2 inches tall to giants at 6 feet tall. They are stunning, sometimes with shimmering foliage and spiraling leaves, and often with beautiful flowers.

Records show that begonias have been used since as early as the 14th century as both a medicinal and culinary plant. From China to Mexico, they have been noted as a source of food, medicine, and vitamin C. The flowers symbolize gratitude and harmony.

Begonia flowers have a very aromatic, bright, citrusy flavor and make a lovely addition to salads. However, only some begonia flowers are edible, so it's best to purchase from a company growing food-grade begonia flowers. See the resource guide on page 153 for my recommended suppliers.

SCARLET BEGONIAS

makes 1 drink

When The Grateful Dead sang to us about "walkin' down Grosvenor Square," we tuned into the story. The song, *Scarlet Begonias*, is about a chance meeting, filled with flirtation. It inspired the ingredients of this cocktail. It's flirty, fruity, and a bit unpredictable.

BEGONIA-INFUSED VODKA

To infuse the vodka, add 1/2 cup of begonia flowers to a jar and cover with vodka. Give them a good shake daily for 5 days. Strain and store in the refrigerator and use within 2 weeks.

2 oz begonia-infused vodka
1 oz apricot cardamom shrub (page 155)
1/2 oz grapefruit juice
1/2 oz sage simple syrup (page 167)
3 dashes lemongrass bitters
3 dashes of Campari

Pour the begonia-infused vodka, shrub, grapefruit juice, and sage simple syrup into a shaker over ice, and shake for 30 seconds. Pour into a chilled glass. Add bitters and Campari. Garnish with a begonia flower.

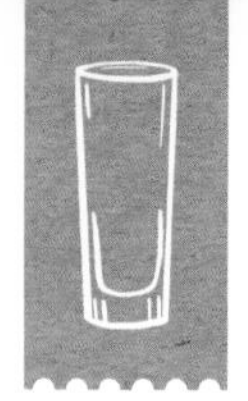

Borage

Borago officinalis

The brilliant blue color of borage is a rare sight to see in the garden. Their star-shaped flowers are delightful and have a flavor that is clean and fresh, similar to that of cucumber. Both the flowers and leaves are edible, the flowers being more palatable. They're most often found frozen in ice cubes for a classic gin and tonic or added as a pop of color to salads.

The English botanist John Gerard mentions an old verse in his book *Of the Historie of Plants* that states a syrup made of the flowers of borage was said to comfort the heart, purge melancholy, and quiet the frantic and lunatic person. This can be attributed to the flower's joyful appearance.

It's been rumored that borage has a cooling effect in drinks. Before the invention of ice, borage was used in a cooling drink called a "claret cup," consisting of wine, water, lemon, sugar, and borage flowers. Sounds just perfect for balmy summer evenings.

NEPENTHEAN FIZZ

makes 1 drink

Pliny the Elder said that borage was the "Nepenthe" mentioned in Homer, which caused forgetfulness. With borage as the featured ingredient, this riff of a classic gin fizz might just clear the mind.

BORAGE-INFUSED GIN

To infuse the gin, add 1/2 cup of borage flowers to a jar and cover with 6 oz of gin. Infuse in the refrigerator for 5 days. Strain and store in the refrigerator. Use within 2 weeks.

2 oz borage-infused gin
1/2 oz borage simple syrup (page 156)
1/2 oz lemon juice
1/2 oz lime juice
1 oz half & half
1 egg white
3 dashes orange blossom water
club soda

Add the egg white to a shaker and shake hard, without ice, for at least one minute. Add the rest of the ingredients to the shaker with ice, leaving out the club soda. Shake hard until chilled. Strain into a tall glass. Carefully top with club soda. Garnish with a borage flower.

Butterfly Pea

Clitoria ternatea

Butterfly pea, also referred to as the blue pea or Asian pigeonwings, is perhaps one of the most magical flowers in this book. The bright indigo petals from the butterfly pea flower have been used as an ingredient in herbal drinks for centuries. In Thailand, a tea simply called "blue tea" is made from butterfly pea flowers, honey, and lemon and is served as an after-dinner drink. Blue tea is said to be high in antioxidants, much like green tea, but is completely caffeine-free.

Most recently, these bright blue flowers have gained popularity for their color-changing abilities. When infused, the flowers turn the mixture the most magnificent, sapphire-blue color. And if that's not fascinating enough, when the pH is altered with an acidic addition (for example lemon juice) the infusion transforms into a vibrant, magenta pink. Magic or science, I still feel like a kid marveling at its color-changing mystique.

BUTTERFLIES ON SATURN

makes 1 drink

The Saturn is possibly my favorite gin-based cocktail. Where rum typically commands the tiki industry, gin offers a lovely balance to the tropical flavors in this classic cocktail. Butterflies on Saturn doesn't veer too much from the original but adds a magical, flower-infused touch.

EMPRESS 1908 GIN

Empress 1908 Gin is an intriguing spirit distilled in Victoria, British Columbia. Its deep violet color is achieved from the addition of butterfly pea blossoms late in the distilling process. Other botanicals used are juniper, Empress tea, grapefruit peel, coriander seed, rose petal, ginger root, and cinnamon bark.

1 1/2 oz Empress 1908 Gin
1/4 oz lemon juice
1/2 oz passion fruit simple syrup (page 165)
1/2 oz sunflower orgeat (page 168)
1/4 oz Velvet Falernum
lemon peel
maraschino cherry

Add lemon juice, passion fruit simple syrup, orgeat, and Velvet Falernum into a shaker with ice, and shake until chilled. Pour into a rocks glass filled crushed ice. Gently float Empress 1908 Gin on top. Garnish with a butterfly pea flower, lemon peel, and a maraschino cherry.

Buzz Button

Acmella oleracea

"Buzz buttons," "Szechuan buttons," "electric daisies," or "toothache plant," whichever name you call them, these are funky little flowers. Popular among ancient tribal communities as a folklore remedy for toothaches, as well as throat and gum infections, the buzz button is commonly used these days as an electrifying addition to both culinary arts and craft mixology.

They have a slightly bitter, grassy flavor that isn't very exciting, but a few seconds after you take even a small bite of one, something very interesting begins to happen in your mouth: a strong numbing or tingling sensation, followed by excessive salivation followed by a cooling feeling in the throat. The sensation only lasts a few minutes but the buzz button is a truly unique sensory experience that goes beyond just taste.

ELECTRIC GUITAR

makes 1 drink

Each sip of the Electric Guitar is bursting with flavor and a mouth feel like you've never experienced before. The cocktail is designed around the effects of the flower, bouncing flavors around on the tongue. The citruses create an effervescent zing and the heat from the jalapeño adds just the right amount of spice. Take one small bite of the buzz button before sipping the drink for a truly one-of-a-kind experience.

BUZZ BUTTON INFUSED-MEZCAL

To infuse the mezcal, add 10 buzz buttons to a jar and add 6 oz of mezcal. Infuse in the refrigerator for 5 days. Strain and store in the refrigerator. Use within 2 weeks.

3/4 oz buzz button infused-mezcal
3/4 oz reposado tequila
1 oz triple sec
1 oz electric mandarin cordial (page 159)
1 oz naval orange juice
1/2 oz lemon juice
1/2 lime juice
2 slices of jalapeño
bittersweet salt (page 155)
orange slice

Rim a glass with the edge of a lime slice and roll into the bittersweet salt.
In the bottom of a shaker, muddle two slices of jalapeño with the citrus juices. Add mezcal, tequila, triple sec, and mandarin cordial and shake with ice until chilled. Strain over a mesh strainer into prepared glass. Garnish with a slice of orange and buzz button.

Carnation

Dianthus caryophyllus

A species of Dianthus, carnations have been cultivated for at least the last 2,000 years. As you can imagine, they're rich with history and folklore — from tales about secret messages sent to and from Victorian admirers, to stories of Oxford University students wearing carnations for good luck on their exams.

The carnation is one of the 130 botanicals which make up the ingredient list for Chartreuse, an enchanting herbal spirit that has been made by Carthusian Monks since 1737. It has been said that Chartreuse was initially developed as an "elixir of long life." Coincidentally, what's great about a carnation flower is its ability to endure. A friend and I once joked that carnations could probably survive an apocalypse and be the last flower living on earth. I like to think that even the monks knew about the longevity of this flower.

LAST FLOWERS

makes 1 drink

The Last Flowers is an ode to carnations and a riff of the classic Chartreuse cocktail, The Last Word. It replaces the traditional ingredients of gin, green Chartreuse, maraschino liqueur, and lime juice with a tropical riff that's still got the classic herbal and fruity complexity.

FALERNUM SYRUP

Falernum, AKA orgeat's spicier cousin, is a popular addition to tiki drinks and is what gives this riff its tropical flair. Its creation dates back to 18th-century Barbados and is produced commercially as a liqueur. *Recipe on page 160.*

3/4 oz London dry gin
3/4 oz green Chartreuse
3/4 oz lime juice
1/2 oz sugar snap pea syrup (page 168)
1/4 oz falernum syrup (page 160)
orange bitters
barspoon of guava juice
pink peppercorn flakes

Pour guava juice into a chilled glass and fill with ice. Add the gin, green Chartreuse, lime juice, sugar snap pea syrup, and falernum syrup to a shaker and shake over ice for 30 seconds. Pour into prepared glass and dash with bitters. Garnish with pink peppercorn flakes and a carnation flower.

Cherry Blossom

Prunus serrulata

The cherry blossom is a flower from many trees of the genus Prunus. All the varieties of cherry blossom trees produce either edible cherries or small, unpalatable fruit. Edible cherries are generally categorized in to two categories: sweet cherries (*Prunus avium)* or sour cherries (*Prunus cerasus)*. The most well-known flowering species is the Japanese cherry, *Prunus serrulata*, which is commonly called *sakura*; however, it falls among the category with inedible fruits.

The cherry blossom is one of the most prominent images throughout Japanese culture. Cherry blossom festivals are held in many parks and castle grounds across Japan. In modern-day Japan, a centuries-old practice called *hanami* is a custom of enjoying the beauty of the cherry blossoms. Under the sakura trees, people have lunch and drink saké in cheerful feasts.

Cherry blossoms are used to flavor many traditional Japanese foods and drinks. They're most commonly preserved with salt and ume plum vinegar for a tea called *sakurayu*.

SAKURA SAKURA

makes 1 drink

Sakura Sakura is an ode to the cherry blossom, using not only one but three ingredients infused with cherry blossoms. Any gin will work but Suntory Roku Gin, which is infused with six natural botanicals, including the sakura flower and sakura leaf, provides the base for the cocktail.

MANCINO SAKURA VERMOUTH is delicious and plays a big part in the flavor of this drink. If you're unable to find it, try infusing dry vermouth with cherries and cherry blossoms for a similar flavor.

1 1/4 oz Suntory Roku Gin
3/4 oz Mancino Sakura Vermouth
1/2 oz Junmai Daiginjo saké
1/4 oz cherry blossom tea (page 157)
3 dashes of cherry bitters

Stir gin, vermouth, saké, and tea together in a mixing glass with ice until chilled. Pour into a chilled glass. Dash bitters and garnish with cherry blossoms.

Geranium

Pelargonium graveolens

Geraniaceae is a family of flowering plants comprised of over 800 different species, divided into seven genera, the largest being Geranium, Pelargonium, and Erodium. Our beloved garden and houseplant cultivars are found in the genus Pelagonium, while the genus Geranium contains the hardy outdoor geranium. The flower gets it's name from the Greek word *geranos* meaning "crane", due to resemblance of the seed heads to the bill of a crane. This is what gives them their other nickname: "cranesbill."

By far the most popular and exciting species of geraniums are the scented varieties. *Pelargonium graveolens*, the rose scented geranium, is often distilled for its essential oil. Its aroma, which comes from the leaves, not the flowers, is sweet, green, and rosy. Scented geraniums are available in many different scents, the most popular being rose- or lemon-scented, but they can even be found in chocolate, orange, almond, or nutmeg!

It's important to note that not all geraniums are edible. Be careful to use *only* scented geraniums, with the exception of citronella.

SWEET AS PIE

makes 1 drink

When developing this drink, I knew I wanted something to highlight scented geranium leaves. Each time I smelled the sweet scent, I kept imagining lemon meringue pie. So Sweet As Pie was developed, with marshmallow sweetness and the kiss of lemons.

GERANIUM-INFUSED VODKA

To infuse the vodka, lightly crush 10 rose-scented geranium leaves between your fingers, releasing their scent. Add to a jar and top with 6 oz of vodka. Infuse in the refrigerator for 5 days. Strain and store in the refrigerator. Use within 2 weeks.

2 oz geranium-infused vodka
3/4 oz limoncello
1/2oz marshmallow simple syrup *(page 163)*
1/2 oz lemon juice
slushee ice

Combine vodka, limoncello, simple syrup, and lemon juice together in a shaker with ice, and shake until chilled. Fill a chilled glass to the brim, almost overfilling with crushed ice. Strain into the glass over the ice, and garnish with a sprig of geranium.

Marigold

Tagetes erecta

Marigolds make up a group of around 55 different species among the genus *Tagetes*. Native to Mexico and Guatemala, their history begins during the 16th century Aztec Empire. Archaeological records show drawings of the flowers represented in early Aztec art. They were considered sacred and were used in religious ceremonies. Additionally, history shows that they were used as an herbal medicine, reported to relieve the hiccups!

In modern-day Mexico, the marigold is known as *cempasúchil* and is seen as an important cultural symbol. They are often found on altars during the Dia de los Muertos celebration, honoring loved ones who have passed. It is believed that the spirits of the dead visit the living during the celebration of Dia de los Muertos, and the marigolds guide the spirits using their strong scent and vibrant color.

ANCHO COCOA

makes 1 drink

MARIGOLD-INFUSED TEQUILA

1 dried ancho chili pepper
3 cinnamon sticks
1/2 cup dried marigold petals
Espolòn Añejo Tequila*

Combine all ingredients together in a large jar and fill with tequila. Give it a good swirl and allow to infuse in the refrigerator for 3-4 days. Strain the tequila into a clean jar and store in a dry place. Use within 2 weeks.

**Any añejo tequila will work here. I just love Espolòn, because at its heart, is a tribute to Mexican culture. Each label tells a story from Mexico's rich history.*

If you're like me, you love your hot cocoa with a little something extra. For me? That's usually spicy additions like cinnamon or ancho chili pepper. Ancho Cocoa takes traditional Mexican Hot Cocoa up a notch by adding in marigold-infused tequila.

6 oz Mexican Hot Cocoa (page 164)
2 oz marigold-infused tequila
3-4 dashes of cacao bitters

Pour hot cocoa and tequila into a mug. Blend with a hand frother. Dash with bitters. Garnish with a marigold flower and a cinnamon stick.

Osmanthus

Osmanthus fragrans

Legends often refer to the osmanthus tree as the "Tree of the Immortals." In one legend, a Jade emperor visits the Moon Palace where he finds a sweet-scented osmanthus tree. Under it he sees a Jade rabbit, grinding osmanthus flowers into an elixir of eternal life. The emperor is entertained with beautiful music and treated to delicious full-moon shaped cakes. Osmanthus flowers now share a symbolic resonance with the moon and people celebrate by eating moon cakes and sharing traditional stories about the moon.

The osmanthus has become a symbol of wealth and luck. Osmanthus, from the Greek words *osma*, meaning "fragrant," and *anthos*, meaning "flower," has a honey-like aroma that has been compared to ripe apricots and peaches. The dried flowers are commonly used to flavor green or black tea or to produce osmanthus-scented jams and desserts. Osmanthus wine is traditionally called reunion wine and is drunk with one's family or during times of celebration.

MOON OVER MANHATTAN

makes 1 drink

Moon Over Manhattan is a riff on the classic Manhattan cocktail. It subs cognac for whiskey and is finished with amaretto and osmanthus tea mist.

OSMANTHUS SWEET VERMOUTH

Sweet vermouth is an ingredient in many classic cocktails. *Vermouth* is the French pronunciation of the German word *Wermut* for "wormwood," which is the primary bittering agent in vermouth. The recipe for sweet vermouth starts with a white wine base, to which botanicals are added for flavor, an additional spirit is added to fortify, and sugar is used to sweeten. *Recipe page 164.*

2 oz cognac
1 oz osmanthus sweet vermouth (page 164)
1/4 oz amaretto
osmanthus tea mist
4 dashes of aromatic bitters
orange twist
maraschino cherries

Stir the cognac, sweet vermouth, and amaretto together in a mixing glass with ice until chilled. Strain into a chilled glass and mist with osmanthus tea. Dash with bitters. Twist orange peel to express oils, and garnish with maraschino cherries.

Peony

Paeonia lactiflora

I like to think that peonies are the goddesses of the garden. Their petals are like a billowy cloud, soft and sweet. They signify romance, elegance, honor, wealth and abundance in the language of flowers. Fittingly so, wouldn't you agree?

Peonies date back to 1000 BCE in the gardens of China. Ancient Chinese texts mention that they were originally revered for their medicinal purposes as well as for flavoring food. To this day, the fallen petals are parboiled and sweetened as a teatime delicacy. It wasn't until the 6th century that peonies became popular plants in imperial gardens.

Today peonies are most often grown as ornamental and cut flowers, and they are one of the most popular flowers for wedding bouquets. They're rewarding cut flowers to grow in your home garden. It's best to pick peonies in early morning before the sun warms the buds. Cut the stems in the bud stage, when they feel soft like a marshmallow. Enjoy them in a vase in a sunny window.

SPRING FEVER

makes 1 drink

When creating this drink, I knew I wanted something that felt fresh like spring and light like a peony. Something that is easy to sip on and delightfully refreshing.

THREE MEADOWS SPIRITS PEONY VODKA

For the cocktail, I used Three Meadows Spirits Peony Vodka, which is an infusion of nine botanicals: peony, jasmine, and geranium to name a few. If you're unable to find it in your region, feel free to sub with your favorite unflavored vodka or try infusing your own with fresh and fragrant peony petals!

2 oz Three Meadows Spirits Peony Vodka
1 oz strawberry peony pink peppercorn cordial (page 167)
1 oz lemon juice
club soda
3–4 dashes grapefruit bitters
rose water
lemon twist
crushed rose petals

Pour vodka, cordial, and lemon juice into a glass, over ice. Gently stir with a barspoon or straw until the outside of the glass becomes frosty. Add more ice and top with club soda. Dash with bitters and mist with rose water. Garnish with a lemon twist and crushed rose petals.

Pineapple Weed

Matricaria discoidea

Pineapple weed or wild chamomile is a weed commonly found blooming along footpaths, cracks in the sidewalk, and other places where almost nothing else grows. It was perhaps the first wildflower I learned to identify, and I would impress anyone wanting to learn about by telling them to crush the buds. For when crushed, the flower buds have a delightfully mild pineapple scent — none like any other flower I've come upon!

Pineapple weed is similar to cultivated chamomile, but it lacks the white petals and only has a yellow or green central cone. Research shows it to have mild sedative effects, helping soothe stress and anxiety, much like chamomile. Also much like chamomile, the most popular way to enjoy pineapple weed is in a tea.

When picking pineapple weed, go for the flowers that are more yellow than green. The greener ones are older and don't have as strong of a flavor. Just be careful where you harvest from to be sure that it is free of toxins.

JUNGLE WEED

makes 1 drink

Playing with the pineapple flavor from pineapple weed, I knew I wanted to start with a cocktail where pineapple was already a key flavor. I created Jungle Weed as a riff on the Jungle Bird cocktail, is a tropical rum cocktail that was created in the early '70s.

PINEAPPLE WEED-INFUSED GOLD RUM

To infuse the rum, add 1/2 cup of pineapple weed flowers to a jar. Add 6 oz of rum. Infuse in the refrigerator for 5 days. Strain and store in the refrigerator and use within 2 weeks.

1 oz dark rum
3/4 oz pineapple weed-infused gold rum
3/4 oz Campari
1/2 oz pineapple weed syrup (page 165)
1 oz pineapple juice
3/4 oz lime juice
pineapple wedge
lime slice

Add the dark rum, pineapple weed-infused rum, Campari, simple syrup, pineapple juice, and lime juice to a cocktail shaker and fill it with ice. Shake vigorously until cold. Strain into a chilled glass. Garnish with a pineapple wedge, pineapple leaves, pineapple weed, and a lime slice.

Violet

Viola odorata

Violets. Spring's splendors. With their delicate and distinctive fragrance, they are among some of my most favorite flowers. A woodland fixture, violets can be found dotting forest floors or popping up in shaded gardens or lawns. In the wild they are found in many different shades of blue, purple, yellow, and white.

The flavor of violets is used in a variety of sweet preparations such as syrups, candies, scones, and marshmallows. Violet essence is used to flavor violet liqueurs. In addition, the violet has proved as a popular source for scents in the perfume industry, known to have a flirty scent unlike any other flower.

Legend says that Romans thought drinking wine from violet blossoms would prevent them from getting drunk. They wore wreaths of violet flowers the morning after to alleviate hangovers. Additionally, it was believed that steeping violet flowers in hot water made a form of tea that helped with heartbreak.

AVIATOR GLASSES

makes 1 drink

The Aviation is a Prohibition-era cocktail consisting of gin, maraschino liqueur, Crème de Violette, and fresh lemon juice. It's enchanting and understated. Aviator Glasses swaps in tequila for gin and lime juice for lemon in an entirely different experience, yet equally as alluring.

CRÈME DE VIOLETTE

Crème de Violette is a delightful liqueur using either natural or artificial violet flower flavoring. It is very floral in flavor which can be overpowering in a cocktail, so use sparingly.

1 1/2 oz blanco tequila
1/2 oz maraschino liqueur
1/4 oz Crème de Violette
3/4 oz lime juice
grapefruit slice

Pour the tequila, maraschino liqueur, Crème de Violette, and lime juice into a shaker over ice and shake for 30 seconds. Strain into a glass over ice and garnish with violet flowers and grapefruit slice.

Bitters & Tinctures

Bitters and tinctures are a fun and easy way to add more depth to your bar cart. Their potent essences provide a boost of flavor and can add that special something that your new libation could be missing. Though both bitters and tinctures were initially developed for medicinal purposes, they are most often used to finish your favorite cocktail these days. Quite simply, the only difference between the two is addition of a bittering agent infused into the bitters such as gentian, angelica root, wormwood, or cassia.

Hawthorn

Crataegus monogyna

There is no other flower, in my opinion, more synonymous with spring than the hawthorn. Often called "mayflower" or "maythorn", the hawthorn is strongly associated with May Day celebrations because it blooms around the first of May. Pink-, white-, and red-blooming hawthorn branches were the prominent flower decorating the May Day maypole. It's also the birth month flower for May.

The fruit of hawthorn, called "haws", are edible raw but are commonly made into jellies, jams, and syrups, made into wine, or used to add flavor to brandy. Hawthorn berries can be used in many recipes, much like other tree fruits, but you should never eat the hawthorn seeds. Just like cherries, apples, or peaches, hawthorn seeds contain cyanide. Just always be sure to remove the seeds before cooking the fresh berries. The Latin name *momogyna* means "one seed" making these fairly easy to remove.

MAY FLOWERS

makes 1 drink

HAWTHORN BITTERS

6 oz 100-proof vodka
1 tbsp hawthorn berries, seeds removed*
2 tsp rose hips
1 tsp ashwaganda root
5 cardamom pods
1/2 vanilla bean

Place the hawthorn berries, rose hips, ashwaganda, and vanilla bean into an 8-oz jar, and top with vodka. Cover and store in a cool, dark place for at least 1 week. After 1 week, add the cardamom and infuse for 1 more day. Strain and reserve the liquid. If you prefer to sweeten your bitters, you can add 1 oz of simple syrup at this point. Store in a dark bottle for up to 1 year.

**Dried berries can also be used if fresh are unavailable.*

Sometimes you're craving something tart, refreshing, AND simple to make. A classic gin & tonic fits the bill. I like my G&T with a little something tart and a little something sweet.

2 oz gin
1/2 oz hawthorn rose cordial (page 161)
1 sprig of rosemary
1/4 oz rose water
3 dashes of hawthorn bitters
tonic water
lime

Muddle the rosemary and rose water in the bottom of a glass. Discard the rosemary. Fill your glass with ice and add the gin and hawthorn rose cordial. Dash with bitters. Top with tonic water and a squeeze of lime.

Lavender

Lavandula spp.

Lavender holds a sacred place in history, which can be traced back nearly 2500 years. It has been long documented as a protective and relaxing herb, from the ancient Egyptians to the early colonists in North America. And it's no wonder — one deep breath of fresh lavender is enough to place you into a deep sense of calm.

Lavender is appropriately associated with the element air, alongside other fragrant flowers. If you've ever been in a field of lavender, just smelling the scent of its flowers blowing in the breeze is meditative and can lull you into deep relaxation. Lavender has been proven to calm nerves, sooth a tired mind, and induce a restful sleep.

Not only does lavender have a rich history in aromatherapy; it also has a strong following as a culinary flavor addition. It can be sweet, sour, and floral, making it an incredibly versatile herb for cooking.

LAVENTINI

makes 1 drink

LAVENDER BITTERS

6 oz 100-proof vodka
1 tbsp dried lavender
2 tsp dried orange peel
1 tsp gentian

Place the lavender, orange peel, and gentian into an 8-oz jar and top with the vodka, just so that it covers the top of the botanicals. Cover the jar and store it in a cool, dark place for at least 1 week. Shake the jar when you think about it, every other day if possible. After 1 week, strain and reserve the liquid. If you prefer to sweeten your bitters, you can add 1 oz of lavender Earl Grey simple syrup at this point. Store in a dark bottle for up to 1 year.

Sexy, strong, and spirit-forward, the Laventini combines all the luxurious flavors of lavender in distinctly different ways, for a fresh and graceful drink.

2 oz lavender-infused gin (page 163)
1/2 oz dry vermouth
1/4 oz Crème de Violette
1/4 oz lavender Earl Grey simple syrup (page 163)
3 dashes of lavender bitters
lemon peel

Stir gin, vermouth, Crème de Violette, and simple syrup together in a mixing glass over ice until chilled. Pour into a chilled glass. Dash bitters and express lemon peel over the drink. Garnish with lemon peel and lavender sprigs.

St. John's Wort

Hypericum perforatum

St. John's Wort flowers are deeply connected to the sun and bring light into our darkest days. They are widely known to elevate mood and ease depression — as well as a variety of sleep disturbances. They can be extremely uplifting during the winter months when sunlight hours are sparse, with the ability to lift the spirits and aid seasonal affective disorder.

Learning to forage for this sunny flower is extremely easy and beneficial. The herb is most potent when used fresh. The scientific name, *Hypericum perforatum*, helps us to identify the plant in the wild. The species name *perforatum* refers to the fact that the leaves of the plant appear to have tiny holes or perforations which can be seen if you hold one of the leaves up to the light. Another key identifying characteristic of St. John's Wort comes from the buds. When crushed between your fingers, they release a bright, ruby red liquid. The flowers can be found abundantly in the wild and often growing near a source of water.

JOHN'S COBBLER

makes 1 drink

ST. JOHN'S WORT TINCTURE

3 cups St. John's Wort flowers
375 ml brandy

Stuff the St. Johns Wort blossoms in a quart-sized jar and fill to the top with brandy. Seal tightly and give it a good shake. The tincture will quickly turn ruby red from the hypericin — the active constituent in St. Johns Wort. Place the jar in a sunny window and shake daily over the next 4 weeks. Strain the blossoms through cheesecloth, reserving the liquid. Pour into amber glass bottles. Store the tincture in a dark place for up to 1 year.

Originating in the early 1800s, The Cobbler was typically a mix of wine, sugar, and fruit poured over crushed or "cobbled" ice, which is where this drink gets its name. John's Cobbler mixes up sherry and port with oranges, spices, and a touch of brandy.

2 oz Olorosso Sherry
1/2 oz brandy
1/2 oz spiced calendula syrup (page 167)
1/2 naval orange
3 barspoons of port
3/4 drops of St. John's Wort tincture

Muddle the orange with the brandy in the bottom of a shaker. Add sherry and calendula syrup and shake with ice. Strain over crushed ice into a glass and top with port and St. John's Wort tincture.

Yarrow

Achillea millefolium

Fossilized yarrow pollen has been found in burial caves that are dated up to 60,000 years old, which gives us clues into yarrow's long and significant history. Yarrow has the ability to assist with almost every system in the body and is often referred to as "nature's Band-Aid." Yarrow gets its botanical name from Achilles, a Trojan war hero who was reputed to have used yarrow to heal wounds on the battlefield.

Yarrow adds a unique and complex element to a cocktail with its sweet sage-like aroma and flavor. It can be a rewarding flower to forage, growing wild in many wooded locations. However, while foraging for yarrow, be absolutely sure to take note of poisonous look-alikes, such as water hemlock or hogsweed, which can be easily recognized after research.

THE STRAIGHT & YARROW

makes 1 drink

YARROW BITTERS

4 oz 100-proof vodka
fresh yarrow blossoms & leaves
2 tbsp chopped gentian
1 or 2 dried figs
1 dried orange peel

Place the gentian, figs, and orange peel into an 8-oz jar and stuff full with the yarrow blossoms and leaves. Pour the vodka into the jar, just so that it covers the top of the herbs and fruit. Cover the jar and store it in a cool, dark place for at least 1 week. Shake the jar when you think about it, every other day if possible. After 1 week, strain and reserve the liquid. Add 1 oz of yarrow simple syrup at this point. Store in a dark bottle for up to 1 year.

Simple yet utterly complex, this cocktail is herbal, nutty, and sweet. The yarrow bitters flawlessly completes the cocktail but can easily be replaced with black walnut bitters in a pinch.

2 oz fig-infused rye (page 159)
3/4 oz yarrow simple syrup (page 169)
1/4 oz Nocino Walnut Liqueur
3–4 yarrow bitters
absinthe wash
lemon peel
fresh fig

Rinse glass with a splash of absinthe and discard. Shake rye, simple syrup, and walnut liqueur over ice, then pour into prepared glass. Add bitters and express lemon peel over the glass. Garnish with a fresh fig and sprig of yarrow.

Salt & Sugar

Salt and sugar are simple ways to add flavor, texture, and balance to a cocktail. Both salt and sugar play important roles in mixology, whether it be in the form of a cube, a dash, a garnish on the rim of a glass, or mixed with water. In this chapter, you'll learn how to use sugar as a technique to flavor a cocktail beyond a simple syrup. I'm focusing on sugar as a cube or garnish, since I'll cover syrups later in the book. And I'll give you a case for salt and why you need to add it to some of your favorite drinks.

Allium

Allium spp.

Allium is a genus of more than 1,000 flowering plants that include onions, garlic, scallions, shallots, leeks, chives, and several ornamental flowers. Carl Linnaeus, a Swedish botanist and physician who formalized binomial nomenclature, first described the genus in 1753. Though the generic name *allium* is from the Latin word for "garlic," it's been said that historians associate the name with the Greek word *aleo*, meaning to "avoid," due to its pungent odor.

Allium has been cultivated for decorative and edible uses as far back as 1594, yet wild varieties of the plant have been foraged for over a thousand years. The flowers come in shades of yellow, light pink, white, and deep purple and have a mild to strong onion flavor.

The importance of various members of allium have been noted throughout history, most importantly onions and garlic. History states that onions are believed to be the most cultivated plant of all time. The flowers are spherical in shape and serve as a sign of harvest for onions and garlic.

THE SALTY SPRITZ

makes 1 drink

Salt deserves a place in traditional mixology, much the same as it does in culinary preparations. It can balance and complete a drink, and even has a finishing textural influence on a drink. In this riff on the White Negroni, the addition of salt tempers the bitterness of the gentian liqueur, Suze, making for a floral and sweet spritz.

CHIVE BLOSSOM SALINE

An unexpected and easy way to enhance the flavor and experience of your cocktails is by adding a few drops of saline. *Find the recipe for Chive Blossom Saline on page 156.*

1 oz gin
1 oz blanc vermouth
1/2 oz Suze
barspoon orange liqueur
Prosecco
2 drops of chive blossom saline
orange peel twist

Stir the gin, blanc vermouth, Suze, and orange liqueur together in a mixing glass with ice until chilled. Strain into an ice-filled glass and top with prosecco. Dash with chive blossom saline solution. Twist orange peel to express oils, and garnish with an orange twist.

Cornflower

Centaurea cyanus

I've always been a sucker for the bright blue blossoms of Cornflowers — sometimes called "Bachelor Buttons." A general legend states the flower was worn by a young man in love, and if the flower faded too quickly, it meant that the lady he fancied didn't return his affections. Whether she was into him or not, the resonance of the deep blue cornflowers is said to attract good vibes.

It's not common you find such a bright shade of blue in nature. Therefore it's no surprise that with the vibrant color of these wildflowers, that they are often used as garnish on top of desserts, drinks, and more. They have a slightly sweet aroma and flavor that reminds me of marshmallows.

SPIN SPIN SUGAR

makes 1 drink

Spin Spin Sugar is a spiral of flavors, hitting everything from tart and bitter to dry and sweet. I often shy away from sugary drinks, but here the sugar isn't too much or over-the-top dessert-like. It adds a perfectly balancing element to the overall drink.

CORNFLOWER SUGAR

1 cup sugar
3 tbsp of cornflower petals*

Pulse petals in a food processor for a few seconds. Combine with sugar in an airtight container and store at room temperature for up to 5 months.

2 oz bourbon
1 oz dry vermouth
1 oz concord grape shrub (page 157)
2 dashes of orange bitters
2 dashes of cardamom bitters
a pinch of cinnamon
lemon slice
lemon peel
sugar dusted grapes

Rub a lemon slice over the rim of a chilled glass, and roll into the cornflower sugar.

Shake bourbon, vermouth, shrub, bitters, and cinnamon over ice and pour into prepared glass. Express a lemon peel over the glass and finish with sugar-dusted grapes.

Dill Flower

Anethum graveolens

Dill is a widely used culinary herb. Its savory and aromatic flavor works well in a variety of dishes but is most commonly known for giving dill pickles their characteristic flavor. If you've ever done your own pickling at home, you have likely used dill flowers in the brine. The flowers pack more flavor than the frilly leaves and seeds do.

The word *dill* comes from the Norwegian word *dilla*, meaning "to soothe or lull." Dating back to about 3000 BCE, many people cultivated it for medicinal qualities, particularly its ability to soothe an ailing stomach. The Egyptians used dill to ward off witches, and the Romans considered it a good-luck symbol.

Modern cultivars are grown not only for their culinary purposes: large dill flowers, or flowering dill, have been grown as a cut flower in recent years. Plus, they're great companion plants in the garden. They attract beneficial insects like ladybugs and praying mantises.

GIN GIN LOE ZER

makes 1 drink

Simple yet unexpected, Gin Gin Loe Zer combines the cucumber-rose infusion of Hendrick's gin with herbal and vegetal spice. It's topped with a pinch of salt, which makes for a flavor explosion in an otherwise unassuming drink.

DILL FLOWER SALT

1/2 cup salt
3 dried dill flower heads

Remove the flowers from the ends of the stems. Pulse in a food processor for a few seconds. Combine with salt in an airtight container and store at room temperature for up to 5 months.

2 oz Hendrick's gin
1/4 oz ginger mint simple syrup (page 161)
1 barspoon aloe vera juice
3 dashes of celery bitters
1 pinch of dill flower salt
4 oz lime seltzer
pickle slices
candied ginger

Combine gin, simple syrup, aloe vera juice, celery bitters, and dill flower salt together in a jar and give it a good swirl. Seal and place in the freezer for 20 minutes. Pour into a chilled glass and add ice. Stir. Top with lime seltzer. Garnish with pickle slices, a piece of candied ginger, and a dill flower.

Pansy

Viola tricolor

The name "pansy" comes from the French word *pensie*, meaning "thought or remembrance." Pansies were so named because the flower resembles a human face, and in late summer it nods forward as if deep in thought. Historically, folks turned to pansies in order to ease their worries. This gave them another nickname: "heartsease."

The frilly cultivated pansies found in garden centers are descendants of wild pansies, *Viola tricolor*, which are commonly called by cute names like "tickle my fancy" or "johnny jump up." They're most often found in three colors: yellow, purple, and white, and they symbolize loving thoughts, trust, and innocence, respectively.

In Shakespeare's *A Midsummer Night's Dream*, a wild pansy is used as the love potion to make people fall in and out of love. If juice from the pansy was placed on a sleeping person's eyelids, they would fall madly in love with the very next person they saw upon opening their eyes.

CALL ME OLD-FASHIONED

makes 1 drink

Call Me Old-Fashioned, but if I had to chose one drink to have forever, this would be it. I can't help it. Someone must have put a spell on me because I've got heart eyes for the Old Fashioned. This riff on the traditional recipe has two kinds of whisky and a pansy sugar cube.

PANSY SUGAR CUBE

Pansies don't have much flavor on their own but they add a nice touch of color to these sugar cubes. Combined with the classic Old Fashioned ingredient, Angostura bitters, these sugar cubes can be used in a variety of cocktails. *Find the recipe on page 165.*

1.5 oz scotch
1.5 oz bourbon
3 dashes Angostura bitters
1 pansy sugar cube (page 165)
orange peel
Luxardo cherry

Place the pansy sugar cube in a chilled glass, and dash it with bitters. Crush the sugar cube with a muddler, then lightly swirl so that the sugar and bitters evenly coat the glass. Add a large, square ice cube, and pour in the scotch and bourbon. Express the oils of an orange peel over the glass, and garnish with a Luxardo cherry and pansy.

Saffron

Crocus sativus

Saffron is a deep purple member of the Crocus family, with three vivid crimson stigmas from which the spice is derived. Ringing up at approximately $5000 per kilogram, saffron is hands down the world's most expensive spice. The high price is primarily because of the labor-intensive harvesting methods required to achieve it. Each flower produces only three stigmas, which must be hand-picked. It requires nearly forty hours of labor to harvest JUST a little over 2 pounds.

Saffron has been coveted throughout history for its use as a spice, dye, perfume, and medicine. It was first cultivated in Greece, where it was eaten to enhance libido, boost mood and improve memory. Just smelling saffron increases levels of serotonin, elevating good feelings all around.

Saffron has found its place the kitchen for its distinct flavor, smell, and vibrant yellow-orange color. The color is what gives it the nickname "sunshine spice." It has a floral, hay-like, peppery flavor that has been widely used in Persian, Indian, European, and Arab cuisines for years. It's not uncommon to find saffron in teas, desserts, and liquors.

MELLOW YELLOW

makes 1 drink

There's nothing mellow about this cocktail, but if you're mad about saffron, this one will fill your cup of tea. Or should I say, cup of champagne? With saffron-infused gin and saffron sugar cubes, this cocktail is a cheerful delight.

SAFFRON CARDAMOM SUGAR CUBE

Sunny yellow and bursting with flavor, these sugar cubes pack a delicious punch in any cocktail. *Find the recipe on page 166.*

1 1/2 oz saffron-infused gin
1/2 oz lemon juice
barspoon rose water
brut Champagne
5 drops of orange bitters
saffron cardamom sugar cube (page 166)
orange peel

In the bottom of a champagne flute, muddle the saffron cardamom sugar cube with bitters, and swirl. Stir together saffron-infused gin, lemon juice, and rose water, in a mixing glass with ice until chilled. Pour into the flute and top with champagne.

Thyme

Thymus vulgaris

Thyme has a long history and is quite possibly my favorite herb to use in the kitchen due to its fragrant, herbaceous, and savory scent. However, history shows that it may not have initially been used as a culinary herb. For example, in ancient Egypt, it was used during the embalming process, and the Romans ate it before a meal to prevent themselves from being poisoned. Today it is used in many things such as herbal medicines, skincare, candy,and liqueurs.

There are a few different suggestions on the origin of the word *thyme*. The Greeks called it an incense plant which, became the word *thymus*, meaning "to fumigate." Other origins state that the word comes from the Greek word *thumos* meaning "expressing the concept of spiritedness or courage."

Native to the eastern Mediterranean, the genus *Thymus* contains about 350 species which are cultivated throughout the world. There are many popular cultivars in addition to common culinary thyme including lemon thyme, citrus thyme, and lavender thyme. All of these vary slightly, creating a unique flavor experience.

ONE-WHEELED RIG

makes 1 drink

The Sidecar is one of my very favorite cocktails to make in my home bar, because it still manages to have that fancy at-the-bar feeling with the sugary rim. One-Wheeled Rig uses thyme flower sugar for an herbal riff on the original.

THYME FLOWER SUGAR

1 cup sugar
3 tbsp of dried thyme flowers

Pulse 1 tbsp of flowers in a food processor for a few seconds. Combine with sugar and remaining flowers. Store at room temperature for up to 5 months.

1 1/2 oz cognac
3/4 oz Cointreau
3/4 oz lemon juice
thyme sprig
thyme flower sugar for rim
orange slice
orange peel

Rim the edge of a chilled glass with an orange slice, then dip the glass into the thyme flower sugar.
Muddle a thyme sprig in the bottom of a shaker with lemon juice. Add the cognac and Cointreau and shake with ice, until chilled. Strain and express an orange peel over the glass.

Cordials, Liqueurs, Syrups, & Shrubs

Cordials, liqueurs, syrups, and shrubs are some of my favorite additions to a cocktail. I absolutely love taking a classic cocktail and creating a riff on it by adding in new flavors. For example, a classic margarita calls for Cointreau, an orange-flavored liqueur. By swapping out this flavor, you get a whole new drink! Cordials, liqueurs, and syrups can be confusing to differentiate as they refer to the same thing in many parts of the world. For the recipes in this book, a cordial will always contain fruit and will not contain alcohol, a liqueur will have an addition of alcohol, and a syrup will be simply a sugar/water preparation. A shrub is something altogether different and will always contain vinegar!

Amaranth

Amaranthus caudatus

Amaranth is believed to have been domesticated as early as 4000 BCE, but evidence of amaranth seeds were found in archaeological sites thousands of years before that. History shows that amaranth was a staple grain for the Inca, Maya, and Aztec civilizations, used primarily as a food crop.

The word *Amaranthus* comes from the Greek word *amarantos*, meaning "unfading," because of its long-lasting blooms and never changing color. Due to this, it was seen as a symbol of immortality and gained importance in religious ceremonies. It was used in ancient rituals to aid spirits in crossing to the other world.

There are three main species of amaranth grown for their edible seeds: *Amaranthus cruenus, Amaranthus hypochondriacus,* and *Amaranthus caudatus.* The flavor of amaranth is best described as nutty and earthy, and is quite delicious when the seeds are popped like popcorn!

THE UNWITHERING

makes 1 drink

When I was starting to work on this cocktail, I kept thinking about the derivative of the word *amaranth*: "unwithering." I knew I wanted something bright in color and turned to blue Curaçao for its rich blue hue. When mixed with yellow Chartreuse, and a pinch of matcha powder, the result is not only colorful but tasty.

PUFFED AMARANTH

Puffed amaranth may be a tiny treat, but it is SO fun and satisfying to create. And it tastes delicious! *Find the recipes for puffed amaranth and puffed amaranth simple syrup on page 166.*

1 1/2 oz coconut-oil washed gin (page 157)
1/2 oz blue Curaçao
1/4 oz yellow Chartreuse
1 oz puffed amaranth simple syrup (page 166)
1/4 oz pineapple juice
1/2 oz lemon juice
a pinch of matcha powder

Add the gin, blue Curaçao, yellow Chartreuse, puffed amaranth simple syrup, pineapple juice, lemon juice, and matcha to a shaker with ice, and shake for 30 seconds. Double strain into a chilled glass, and garnish with an amaranth flower.

Basil

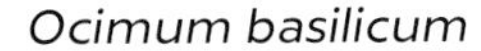

Ocimum basilicum

Basil is one of the most widely used culinary herbs in the world. A member of the mint family with a characteristic square, hairy stem, and over 30 distinct varieties, basil is one the most diverse herbs in aroma and symbolism. Known as the king of herbs, the name "basil" comes from the Greek *basilikón phutón* meaning "royal/kingly plant." Perhaps that's because of it's long-renowned history for uses in both culinary preparations and folklore.

Basil is said to have originated in Southeast Asia, though it's in Italy where we find basil to be most significant. Basil had a bit of a love-hate relationship through Roman history. It was once regarded as a symbol of hatred, and Romans believed the most potent basil could only be grown if one sowed the seed while ranting and swearing. Most recently, basil is seen as a token of love and has had that sentiment ever since.

As beautiful as basil flowers are, they're a signal that your plant is going to seed, rather than growing more leaves. It's best to pick them off the plant and enjoy them in the kitchen. Pinching the flowers helps keep the plant growing.

BRAMBLE ON

makes 1 drink

The Bramble is a cocktail created in the 1980s by bartender Dick Bradsell. The drink name comes from the fact that blackberry bushes are called "brambles." Bramble On takes the cleverly simple original and swaps gin with berry-infused vodka, and then adds basil flower for an herbal touch.

CRÈME DE MÛRE AU BASILIC

Crème de Mûre, or blackberry liqueur, is incredibly simple to make at home. My version adds basil to offset the sweet. *Find the recipe on page 158.*

2 oz marionberry vodka
3/4 basil flower-infused dry vermouth (page 155)
1/2 oz lime juice
1/2 oz Crème de Mûre au Basilic (page 158)
6 blackberries
1/4 oz basil flower syrup (page 155)
3-4 dashes of Angostura bitters

Muddle blackberries with lime juice in a shaker. Add vodka, vermouth, Crème de Mûre au Basilic, and basil flower syrup with ice, and shake until chilled. Strain over a mesh strainer and dash with bitters. Garnish with a basil flower.

Black Locust

Robinia pseudoacacia

I still remember the very first time I stumbled upon locust flowers. I was stopped in my tracks by the intoxicating scent surrounding me. The trees above me were in bloom with aromatic clusters of white flowers that smelled like honey perfume. Years later I discovered their edibility and couldn't wait till spring to pluck the sweet blossoms straight from the branches.

Native to the Appalachian Mountains, black locust trees have naturalized throughout the country. They have one of the hardest woods in North America. It is believed that Native Americans moved this useful tree from the mountains to the coastal plains for its excellence as bow wood.

The flowers themselves and the tiny stems around them are fine to eat, but the rest of the plant — the leaves, the bark, and the wood — is toxic. Be sure to strip the flowers from the stems before using them.

TOAST TO SUMMER

makes 1 drink

LOCUST FLOWER SORBET

2 cups locust blossoms*, stems removed
2 cups sugar
2 cups water
zest and juice of one lemon

In a large bowl mash the locust blossoms with 1/2 cup of sugar to form a paste, and set aside. Bring the remaining sugar and water to a boil over medium heat. Once the sugar is dissolved, stir in the locust blossom paste and reduce the heat to a simmer. Simmer for 10 minutes. Add in lemon zest and simmer 5 minutes more. Remove from heat and cool completely.
Strain through a coffee filter into a freezer-safe container. Freeze for about 4 hours, or until firm.

Toast to Summer is inspired by those warm days just before spring turns to summer, when the locust blossoms are in peak bloom. Their sweet scent fills the air and promises of warm days ahead.

1 oz London dry gin
1 scoop of locust flower sorbet
brut Champagne

Pour gin to a chilled glass. Add a scoop of sorbet and top with Champagne. Garnish with fresh locust blossoms.

**If you're unable to forage locust blossoms, sub elderflower here for an equally delightful treat!*

Calendula

Calendula officinalis

Calendula flowers have a strong connection to the sun and the calendar. First cultivated by the ancient Romans, the name *calendula* is Latin for "the first" or "little clock" because it tends to bloom in accordance with the calendar. Its petals range in shades of orange and yellow, and when plucked clockwise, calendula is the traditional "he loves me, he loves me not" flower.

Early herbal practitioners relied on calendula's sunny disposition and gentle immune-boosting properties for protection against the damp cold of winter. It has been prized for its effect on dry skin but also works wonders on minor rashes, cuts, insect bites, wounds, and so much more.

A calendula infusion was thought to give one a healthy, sunny glow that would draw admiration and respect from one's community. It was used as a coloring agent in soups and broths, and the petals of the flowers were used in puddings, dumplings, and even wine.

CALENDULADA

makes 1 drink

The history of when and where the Piña Colada originated is debatable, but one mention of the cocktail and you're instantly transported to a beachside bar. When developing this drink, I wanted a nod to the original, with bitter and spice elements to balance the sweet. Calendulada is still much like the original, with just a little more sophistication.

SPICED CALENDULA SYRUP

With warm flavors from clove, allspice, and cinnamon sticks, this might just be your favorite new simple syrup. *Find the recipe on page 167.*

1 oz white rum
1/2 oz overproof rum
1/2 oz Suze
3/4 oz lime juice
3/4 oz pineapple juice
1/2 oz cream of coconut
1/2 oz spiced calendula syrup (page 167)
6 dashes Angostura bitters
pineapple slice

Dash bitters into the bottom of a glass and fill with ice to the very top. Shake remaining ingredients in a shaker with ice until chilled. Pour into the prepared glass. Garnish with a calendula flower, a pineapple slice, and pineapple leaves.

Chrysanthemum

Chrysanthemum spp.

Chrysanthemum flowers were first cultivated in China as far back as the 15th century BCE, and now there are approximately 200,000 different cultivated varieties. As an herb, it was believed to have the power of life. Chinese chefs added the flowers to meals that needed a floral hint to enhance the flavor. Chrysanthemum tea soon became popular in Chinese culture and is still drank widely throughout Asia and the rest of the world.

Chrysanthemums have earned the name "Queen of Fall Flowers", due to the time of their bloom. They come into their prime in the fall when most flowers are fading away. In fact, the Chinese word for chrysanthemum literally translates to "October Flower."

All species of chrysanthemum are edible and have flavors ranging from sweet to peppery or bitter. The most commonly used in sweet infusions, such as traditional Asian chrysanthemum tea, comes from the yellow or white flowers of *Chrysanthemum morifolium* or *Chrysanthemum indicum.*

MUM'S THE WORD

makes 1 drink

Mum's The Word is my take on the famous prohibition-era cocktail Bees Knees, with a Chinese flavor twist. Many prohibition-era cocktails were sweetened with honey as a way to hide the scent and flavor of poor-quality homemade spirits. Mum's The Word gets honey by way of Chrysanthemum Honey Liqueur, a delightful flavor infusion from my friends at KOVAL Distillery.

**If you're feeling ambitious and would like to try making your own Chrysanthemum Honey Liqueur, follow the recipe for Forsythia Honey Liqueur on page 160 and sub dried chrysanthemum flowers.*

2 oz London dry gin
*1 oz KOVAL Chrysanthemum Honey Liqueur**
1/2 oz yuzu essence
1/2 oz schisandra simple syrup (page 158)
1/4 oz kumquat simple syrup (page 163)
candied kumquats (page 156)

Combine all ingredients together in a shaker with ice, and shake until chilled. Pour into a glass and garnish with candied kumquats and chrysanthemum petals.

Elderflower

Sambucus nigra

The elder tree is filled with folklore, superstition, and medicinal powers — altogether perhaps more than any other plant. Thought of as a protective tree, the elder was believed to keep evil spirits from entering the house. The elder is associated with fortitude and strength, yet under its protective canopy of light and airy flowers, one might find a sense of inner peace.

The use of elderflowers in culinary preparations was popular in northwestern Europe. Delicious pancakes were made by dipping the fresh-picked elderflower blossoms in batter, frying them, and sprinkling them with sugar. However, it's an infusion of the honey-scented blossoms for cordials, liqueurs, and tea where they really gained their popularity.

The berries from the elder tree have been used in traditional medicine by native peoples and herbalists for cold and flu symptoms. It's important to note that the elderberries in their raw state, as well as the leaves, bark, and stems from the elder tree, are toxic and should never be eaten.

UNDER MY UMBRELLA

makes 1 drink

It's said that under the umbrella of the elderflower tree, one can get lost in their thoughts. One sip of Under My Umbrella and suddenly it's summer, with all its charm and delight.

ELDERFLOWER LIQUEUR

Elderflower liqueur may possibly be one of the most delightful flavors that I've ever come across. It's floral, of course, but also lightly citrusy and tart. There are many delicious versions in production today, but this homemade version is satisfyingly delicious! *Find the recipe on page 159.*

2 oz reposado tequila
1/2 oz elderflower liqueur (page 159)
1/2 oz elderflower simple syrup (page 159)
3/4 oz lime juice
2 cups of ice
coarse sea salt
lime wheel

Prepare your glass by rubbing the rim with a lime and coating it with salt. Place in the freezer until ready to use. In a blender, combine tequila, elderflower liqueur, simple syrup, lime juice, and ice. Blend well. Pour into your prepared glass and garnish with a lime wheel.

Fennel Blossom

Foeniculum vulgare

Fennel has no friends when it comes to companion planting. Though when it when it comes to culinary creativity, fennel is definitely a friend! With a taste similar to licorice, the bright yellow umbel shaped flower clusters are often used as flavoring in cooking due to their unique taste. Fennel is one of the three main herbs used in the preparation of absinthe, (alongside wormwood and green anise), and gives absinthe its characteristic black-licorice flavor.

Fennel is native to the Mediterranean region. It was prized by ancient Greeks and Romans, who used it as medicine, food, and insect repellent. It was said to promote strength and longevity. A fennel tea was believed to give courage to the warriors prior to battle. According to Greek mythology, Prometheus used a giant stalk of fennel to carry fire from Mount Olympus to Earth.

DEWY DAIQUIRI

makes 1 drink

HONEYDEW FENNEL CORDIAL

1 cup sugar
1 cup water
1 honeydew melon, chopped
1/2 cup fresh fennel blossoms

Combine sugar and honeydew in a bowl and stir until the sugar completely covers the fruit. Refrigerate overnight. Pour the honeydew and any juices released into a pot with water, and bring to a gentle simmer over medium heat. Once the sugar has dissolved completely, remove from the heat. Add the fennel blossoms, cover, and steep for 20 minutes. Strain the solids and cool completely before using. Store in the refrigerator for up to one week.

One of my favorite ways to finish a daiquiri is with a mist of absinthe for a licorice-flavor finish. The addition of fennel, when paired with the light, subtle flavor of honeydew melon, makes for a daiquiri that's dewy and fresh.

1 1/2 oz white rum
1/2 oz pot still rum
3/4 oz lime juice
3/4 oz honeydew fennel cordial
absinthe mist

Add white rum, pot still rum, lime juice, and honeydew fennel cordial to a shaker with ice, and shake until chilled. Strain into a chilled glass and mist with absinthe. Garnish with a fennel flower.

Forsythia

Forsythia suspensa

Forsythia was first cultivated in the late 1800s and has been grown in gardens for its bright, showy yellow flowers blooming early in the spring. But forsythia was documented in ancient medicine long before that. *Forsythia suspensa* originated in China and is considered one of the 50 fundamental herbs in Chinese herbology with many healing properties to its name.

Forsythia has gained popularity as one of the earliest bloomers. It's such a show to see those joyful blooms after a long winter. Fittingly so, the sentiment of anticipation is associated with forsythia. Folklore says we should expect three more snowfalls after their initial bloom. After a long, hard winter, the thought of more snow makes me batty. But as the saying goes, "good things come to those who wait." The anticipation of spring is worth it — even if we have a bit more winter to trudge through!

SPRING STING

makes 1 drink

Spring Sting is like those first days of spring when the sunshine has you dreaming of summer, but there's still a chill in the air. The sting comes from reposado tequila and muddled jalapeño.

FORSYTHIA HONEY LIQUEUR

The secret to coaxing out the sweet fragrance of forsythia flowers is allowing them to wilt slightly. AI find that a few hours or even overnight is the perfect amount of time for them to release their sweet honey-like scent. *Find the recipe for forsythia honey liqueur on page 160.*

1 oz reposado tequila
1 oz forsythia honey liqueur (page 160)
1 oz lemon juice
2 slices of jalapeño
lemon peel

In a shaker, lightly muddle jalapeño slices with lemon juice. Add tequila and forsythia honey liqueur, and shake over ice until chilled. Strain into a chilled glass and express a lemon peel over glass. Garnish with a sprig of forsythia flowers.

Goldenrod

Solidago spp.

Solidago, commonly called "goldenrods," is a genus of around 120 different species. *Solidago* means "whole" in Latin and is thought to be a reference to its reputed healing powers. The sweet anise-like goldenrod flowers were used as a tea by Native Americans to relieve cramps and for general anti-inflammatory purposes. They chewed the leaves to relieve sore throats and toothaches.

Solidago is about happiness and, in some places, is considered a sign of good fortune. It's also said to open our intuition to a way of greater clairvoyance. A legend states that if you concentrate on what you're looking for while holding goldenrod in your hand, it will point in the direction of treasure or your true love.

You can find goldenrod growing in prairies, savannas, and riversides, and all throughout the Americas. Even though it is considered a weed in many parts of America, it is recognized as the state flower for three states: Kentucky, Nebraska, and South Carolina.

THE CLAIRVOYANT

makes 1 drink

GOLDENROD TURMERIC HONEY SYRUP

1/2 cup honey
1/2 cup water
1/4-inch knob of turmeric, sliced
1/2 cup of goldenrod blossoms

Combine the honey, water, and turmeric in a small pot, and bring to a gentle simmer over medium heat. Once the sugar has dissolved completely and the syrup has slightly thickened, remove from the heat. Add the goldenrod flowers, cover, and steep for 20 minutes. Strain solids, reserving the syrup. Cool completely before using. Store in the refrigerator for 1 week.

One who sees clearly. Extrasensory perception. The Clairvoyant. No promises that this drink will give you a glimpse into the future, but it's fun to think about the buried treasure you could find.

3/4 oz rye
1/2 oz yellow Chartreuse
1/2 oz goldenrod turmeric honey syrup
1/2 oz mango juice
1/2 oz lemon juice
mango slices

Add rye, yellow Chartreuse, honey syrup, mango juice, and lemon juice to a shaker with ice, and shake until chilled. Strain into a prepared glass and garnish with a slice of mango and goldenrod flowers.

Hops

Humulus lupulus

If you've ever seen a hop vine, you can understand how they've gotten their name, *Humulus lupulus*. The word *lupulus* is Latin for "small wolf." This refers to the plant's tendency to strangle other plants, much like a wolf does a sheep. They're fiercely wild, tangled together, and can grow to a massive height of 20 feet.

Since their first documentation in beer brewing during the 9th century, hops have become the darling of the craft beer industry. The part of the plant used in brewing beer is the hop flower, with aromatic resins tucked inside the cones.

Prized by brewers and loved by beer aficionados, hops are perhaps the single most important element for adding flavor to beer, contributing flavors from citrusy, floral, pine, bitter, to fruity flavors.

HOPPED & SOUR

makes 1 drink

I felt pretty fancy the first time I ordered a Whiskey Sour from a bar. The bartender handed it to me, all frothy and delicious looking and instantly I was hooked. It packs a big punch for such a simple ingredient list — the zing from the citrus balancing the bourbon so nicely. The Hopped & Sour doesn't veer too much from the original, but I love the idea of adding another citrus element by way of the characteristic flavors from a classic Northwest IPA.

IPA SIMPLE SYRUP

Reduce the water in a simple syrup by half, and swap in your favorite citrus-forward, hop-filled IPA in this flavorful twist. *Find the recipe on page 162.*

2 oz bourbon
3/4 oz IPA simple syrup (page 162)
3/4 oz lemon juice
1 egg white
3 dashes of Angostura bitters
hopped bourbon cherries (page 162)

Dry-shake the egg white vigorously for 30 seconds. Add ice bourbon, simple syrup, and lemon juice to the shaker, and shake for another 10 seconds. Strain into a chilled glass. Dash with bitters and garnish with a hopped bourbon cherry.

Lilac

Syringa vulgaris

I still remember the first time I smelled the magical scent of a lilac. Years ago, a friend brought me some cut flowers from a bush in her yard, and I was instantly smitten. I couldn't stop burying my face in the light purple blossoms, and years later I'm still enamored by their elegance and the memories they induce.

Lilac is believed to have originated on the Balkan peninsula, where it grows on rocky hills. It was noted to have been cultivated in the late 16th century as a garden favorite. Today there are over 1,000 lilac varieties in existence in shades of pale purple and pink to bright white or deep magenta.

The scent of the lilac is ephemeral— it's fleeting, then quickly fades. When the lilacs are in bloom, their scent clings to the air. It's something I want to hold onto for as long as possible. Be sure to pick lilacs in the early morning to retain their sweetest scent.

LILAC COLORED GLASSES

makes 1 drink

LILAC SIMPLE SYRUP

1 cup water
1 cup sugar
1 cup fresh lilac blossoms, pulled from the stem

Combine water and sugar in a small pot, and bring to a gentle simmer over medium heat. Once the sugar has dissolved completely and the syrup has slightly thickened, remove from the heat. Add the lilac blossoms, cover and steep for 20 minutes. Strain solids, reserving the syrup. Cool completely before using. Store in the refrigerator for up to 1 week.

The taste of spring — fleeting and seemingly spontaneous. Sweet honey from lilac and a sharp bite from rhubarb combine with pisco for a breezy delight.

2 oz pisco
1/2 oz lilac simple syrup
1/2 oz rhubarb simple syrup
(page 166)
1/4 oz lemon juice
egg white
jalapeño bitters

Dry-shake the egg white vigorously for 30 seconds. Add pisco, lilac syrup, rhubarb syrup, and lemon juice with a handful of ice to the shaker, and shake for 30 seconds more. Strain into a chilled glass and top with 3-4 drops of bitters.

Nasturtium

Tropaeolum majus

The name *nasturtium* comes from the Latin words *nasus tortus* meaning "nose twister." This is the face many people make after tasting the spicy, bittersweet petals of nasturtium. It is an easily-grown annual with colors ranging from bright shades of red, orange, and yellow to pastel shades of yellow and white.

They were introduced by the Spaniards to Europe in the 1500s where they became a symbol of power. Nasturtium is now found in abundance in French Royal Gardens, though it was important to many civilizations. In particular, the Incas believed that nasturtium gave them vigor and vitality, and they would eat it before battle. Fittingly so, the nasturtium is known as the "flower of heroes."

All of the above-ground parts of the plant are edible. The flowers have a slightly peppery taste and add a pop of color to a meal. The leaves can replace greens in sandwiches or salads, and even the unripe seed pods can be harvested and dropped into spiced vinegar, similar to a caper.

BOTANY SPRITZ

makes 1 drink

NASTURTIUM CORDIAL

1 cup sugar
1/2 cup water
25 nasturtium petals
1 sprig of lemon thyme
1 orange, sliced

Combine sugar and water together in a pot, and bring to a gentle simmer over medium heat. Once the sugar has dissolved completely, remove from the heat. Add the nasturtium petals, thyme, and orange slices, cover, and steep overnight. Strain the solids and cool completely before using. Store in the refrigerator for up to 1 week.

Botany Spritz is a riff on the classic Italian aperitif, the Aperol Spritz. It adds a bit of peppery bite from the nasturtium as well as the berry richness from sloe gin.

2 oz Aperol
1/2 oz sloe gin
1/2 oz orange vanilla shrub (page 164)
1/2 oz nasturtium cordial
Prosecco
orange wheel

Add ice to a chilled glass. Pour Aperol, sloe gin, shrub, and cordial over the ice. Swirl with a barspoon. Top with Prosecco. Garnish with an orange wheel and nasturtium flowers.

Oregon Grape Flower

Mahonia aquifolium

Oregon grape is one of my favorite Pacific Northwest native plants. The flowers are such a cheerful yellow and have the most wonderful honey-like fragrance. They produce a bitter fruit, which, when sweetened, can be cooked into pie fillings, jellies, jams, and can even be made into a delicious wine.

In addition to being used as a food source, Oregon grape has wonderful medicinal properties; the entire plant can be used, from the flowers to the roots! Not only is it high in antioxidants and vitamin C, but much of Oregon grape's use is based on its primary active ingredient, the alkaloid berberine, which is found in the flowers, fruit, stems, and roots.

When given as a gift, the Oregon grape flowers are most commonly presented to the recipient as a way of telling him or her that they are loved for who they are. That they are enough. Which for the small stature of the flower, is a powerful affirmation.

LOST IN THE WOODS

makes 1 drink

MAHONIA FIR SIMPLE SYRUP

1 cup water
1 cup sugar
1 cup of Douglas fir needles
1/4 cup of Oregon grape flowers*
zest from 1 lemon

Combine water and sugar in a small pot, and bring to a boil over medium heat. Once the sugar has dissolved completely and the syrup has slightly thickened, remove from the heat and stir in the Oregon grape flowers and lemon zest. Steep for 15 minutes. Allow to cool slightly before straining the solids, reserving the syrup. Cool completely before using. Store in the refrigerator for 1 week.

1 1/2 oz fir-infused vodka (page 160)
1/2 oz green Chartreuse
1 oz fresh green juice (page 161)
1/2 oz mahonia fir simple syrup
3 kumquats
3-4 dashes of anise bitters

Lightly muddle the kumquats, releasing their juice. Add vodka, Chartreuse, green juice, and simple syrup to the shaker, and shake over ice until chilled. Pour over crushed ice and dash with bitters. Garnish with kumquats, Oregon grape flowers, and pineapple leaves.

**If Oregon grape flowers don't grow in your region, substitute with elderflower or calendula.*

Passionflower

Passiflora incarnata

Native from the Southeast United States to Argentina and Brazil, the passion flower is well known as an herbal remedy. In the late 1500s, a Spanish doctor was the first to record the use of passionflower when visiting Peru, where passion flower has long been used for calming a restless mind. There are over 500 species of *Passiflora*, but *Passiflora incarnata*, grown as a medicinal herb, and *Passiflora edulis*, grown for its sweet and tart fruit, are among the most popular.

With a strong correlation to Christ and Christianity, Spanish missionaries used the passionflower as a visual to teach and represent the Passion of Christ, or Christ's crucifixion. The three stigmas represented the nails of crucifixion, the coronal filaments were the crown of thorns, the five stamens were the wounds, and the ten sepals were representative of the ten disciples.

MARACUJÁ BATIDA

makes 1 drink

PASSIONFLOWER LIME CORDIAL

3/4 cups water
1 cup sugar
1/4 cup dried passionflower
1 tsp citric acid
zest and juice from 4-5 limes

Bring water to a gentle simmer in a saucepan, and add citric acid and sugar. Once the sugar is fully dissolved, remove from the heat. Add the dried passionflower and steep for 10 minutes. Strain and return syrup to the pot. Add lime zest and juice and bring back to a gentle simmer for 2 minutes. Remove from the heat, cover and infuse overnight.
Strain through a cheesecloth, reserving the liquid. Keep refrigerated for up to 3 months.

Maracujá Batida features both passionflower and passion fruit for a sweet and sour take on a traditional Brazilian Batida. In Portuguese *batida* means "shaken" or milkshake and *maracujá* means "passion fruit."

2 oz cachaça
1 oz coconut milk
1 oz lime juice
1/2 oz passion fruit syrup (page 165)
1/2 oz passionflower lime cordial
Amontillado sherry rinse

Pour a splash of amontillado sherry into the glass, rinse, and discard. Shake cachaça, coconut milk, lime juice, passion fruit syrup, and passionflower lime cordial with ice until frothy. Pour over pebbled ice into prepared glass, and top with fresh-grated nutmeg.

Safflower

Carthamus tinctorius

Safflower is one of humanity's oldest crops. It was discovered through a chemical analysis indicating that textiles from ancient Egypt were dyed from safflower, which yields a yellow or red dye, depending on the preparation. This gave it the nickname "Dyer's Saffron." These textiles dated back to the Twelfth Dynasty, or approx 1991 BCE–1802 BCE. Even garlands made from safflowers were found in the tomb of the pharaoh Tutankhamen.

Most safflower is cultivated for its seed oil, which is a rich source of unsaturated fatty acids. It has a neutral flavor that pairs well with many dishes and cuisines. Safflower is often found in mixed tea blends for a fun pop of red color and an added boost of antioxidants, but on its own it is helpful for those with anxiety or stress.

PERA DE FUEGO

makes 1 drink

SAFFLOWER SMOKED CINNAMON SIMPLE SYRUP

1 cup water
1 cup sugar
2 cinnamon sticks
10 cloves
1 small knob of ginger
1 tbsp safflower petals

Gently warm sugar in a small pot over medium-low heat, being careful that it does not stick to the bottom of the pan. When it begins to brown, add water and bring to a gentle simmer. Once the sugar has dissolved completely, remove from heat. Place two cinnamon sticks under a flame until smoking, and drop them into the syrup. Add the cloves and ginger, cover, and steep for 30 minutes. In the last 5 minutes, add the safflower petals. Strain out the solids and cool completely before using. Store in the refrigerator for up to 1 week.

Pera de Fuego begins with a cinnamon-infused tequila for a warm depth and flavor explosion balanced by the softness of pear liqueur. It's finished with an unexpected hint of smoky spice.

1 1/2 oz cinnamon–infused reposado tequila (page 157)
1 oz pear liqueur
1 oz safflower–smoked cinnamon simple syrup
1 barspoon of hazelnut orgeat (page 161)
3 dashes of barrel–aged bitters
sliced pears
cinnamon stick

In a shaker, combine the cinnamon-infused tequila, pear liqueur, safflower-smoked cinnamon simple syrup, and hazelnut orgeat, and shake vigorously for 20 seconds. Pour into a chilled glass. Dash with bitters. Garnish with sliced pears and a smoking cinnamon stick.

Sunflower

Helianthus annuus

Helianthus annuus, the common sunflower, is a large, cheerful flower grown as a crop for its edible oil and edible fruits. With their tall, stately stature and bright, sunny faces, sunflowers make a welcome addition to any garden. There are many cultivars in various colors and sizes.

The sunflower was first cultivated by Native Americans over 3,000 years ago. It was used as a food crop and a dark blue-black dye, and it was planted as a "fourth sister" to the three sisters companion planting of corn, beans, and squash. The Incas used it as a symbol to represent their solar deity. Perhaps this was because of the magical way sunflowers turn their heads to face the sun as it moves from east to west.

Everything from the sprouts and young flowering buds to the petals and dried seeds can be eaten. The petals of a sunflower are lovely in a salad, but it's the seeds that really shine. They can be eaten raw, steeped into tea, or ground into a delicious butter.

GOOD DAY, SUNSHINE

makes 1 drink

Good Day, Sunshine gets a boost of flavor from the sunflower orgeat. Perfectly smooth, fruity and nutty, this drink might transport you straight to the beach.

SUNFLOWER ORGEAT

Orgeat, an important ingredient in the Mai Tai and many other Tiki cocktails, is traditionally made from almonds, but I love exploring other nuts and seeds. The sunflower orgeat is nothing short of delicious. *Find the recipe on page 168.*

2 oz brown-butter-washed rum (page 156)
1.5 oz sunflower orgeat (page 168)
1/2 cup frozen pineapple
1/2 cup frozen banana
1 lime, juiced
2 pieces of candied ginger
4 dashes of orange bitters
1 pinch of nutmeg
pineapple wedge

Place all ingredients into a blender and blend on high until smooth. Garnish with a broiled pineapple slice, pineapple leaves, and a sunflower.

Sweet William

Dianthus barbatus

Sweet William is one of the 300+ species in the genus Dianthus. A cousin to carnations and garden pinks, Sweet William gained popularity in gardens, and several cultivars have been developed. It's not unusual to find Sweet William in shades of white, red, pink, and purple, as well as many variegated varieties.

A symbol of gallantry, the flower has been surrounded by many stories and myths. One story claims the origin of the name comes from the time of William the Conqueror, when the flowers covered the hills where he was victorious.

Sweet William petals can be eaten raw and have a spicy, clove-like flavor. The petals, when pulled away from the bitter green calyx, can be used as a garnish for deserts, or even added to jams, jellies, syrups, and more.

THE BOHEMIAN

makes 1 drink

DIANTHUS CLOVE SHRUB

1 cup sugar
1 cup white vinegar
50 fresh dianthus petals
20 cloves

Place the petals into a clean jar. Allow them to slightly wilt, then add cloves and sugar to the jar and give it a good shake to coat the petals in sugar. Place in the refrigerator for 30 minutes until flowers and sugar have thoroughly combined. Add white wine vinegar to the petal mixture, shake again, and place back into the refrigerator to steep for 2 days. Strain and store in the refrigerator for up to 6 months.

2 oz of blanco tequila
1 1/2 oz dianthus clove shrub
1/2 oz orange sea salt cordial (page 164)
1/4 oz bergamot liqueur
3 dashes of grapefruit bitters

Add tequila, dianthus clove shrub, orange sea salt cordial, and bergamot liqueur to a shaker, and shake over ice until chilled. Strain into a chilled glass and dash with bitters. Garnish with fresh dianthus flowers.

Wild Rose

Rosa nutkana

Wild roses grow in many parts of the Americas, but the northwest-native Nooka Rose, perhaps best know for its pink blooms, intoxicating scent, and red rose hips, is among the favorites. The beautiful blossoms are said to be found where the forest meets the field, road, or shore.

Native Americans used the Nooka Rose as food and medicine. The flowers were dried and used in teas or healing poultices, and the edible hips were used to make tea, jam, and jellies. The hips are an abundant source of vitamin C. During the first and second world war, people were advised to prepare them as a vitamin supplement. It should be noted that the seeds shouldn't be eaten, as they can be irritating to the stomach.

When foraging for wild roses, be sure not to pick all the petals from a single flower, leaving 1-2 petals for happy pollinators.

THE WILD ROSE

makes 1 drink

WILD ROSE CORDIAL

2 cups water
2 cups sugar
2 cups dried wild rose petals
2 tbsp citric acid
1 tbsp lemon juice
1 orange, sliced thin

Bring water and sugar to a boil in a saucepan, and then remove from heat. Stir to fully dissolve the sugar. Add the wild rose petals, citric acid, lemon juice, and orange slices into the sugar and water syrup. Cover and infuse overnight. Pour the mixture through a fine mesh strainer and bottle. Keep refrigerated for up to 3 months.

Summertime: a time to revel in the treats of the season. Each summer, I head to my favorite local river-side haunt to pick wild roses. Their scent is undeniably intoxicating and this cocktail really captures their essence.

2 oz gin
1 oz wild rose cordial
3 dashes of wild rose bitters *(page 169)*
3 dashes of grapefruit bitters

Shake gin and cordial over ice, then pour into a chilled glass. Dash with bitters and express a lemon over the glass. Garnish with a wild rose.

Floral Water & Tea

Floral water and tea add a fragrant and inviting flavor to a cocktail. What puts these into a chapter together is straightforward: they both include a water infusion in some form. Floral waters, in the simplest terms, are water that has a floral aroma. They're used to enhance or finish a cocktail. Teas are often used as a base for hot drinks but can also be expanded into syrups, infusions, or even more.

Chamomile

Matricaria chamomilla

When I imagine peace in the form of a flower, the first one that comes to mind is chamomile. It's like a deep, renewing breath, leaving you feeling completely at ease. With its soothing, airy fragrance, it's no surprise that chamomile flowers have found their way into many remedies for bringing peace to the mind.

A sun-loving plant, chamomile dates back thousands of years to ancient Egypt, where it was considered a sacred gift from the sun god, Ra. Hieroglyphics show that chamomile was used in skincare by Egyptian noblewomen. Both the Egyptians and the ancient Romans used chamomile in tea and other beverages.

It's been noted that chamomile before bedtime helps one to fall asleep easily and rest soundly. There are two species of chamomile commonly used to do so: German chamomile, found in dried tea, and Roman chamomile, used in aromatherapy.

CHAMOMILE TODDY

makes 1 drink

CHAMOMILE HONEY SYRUP

1 cup orange blossom honey
1 cup water
1/2 cup dried chamomile flowers
1 inch piece of lemon peel

Combine the honey and water in a small pot, and bring to a gentle simmer over medium heat. Once the honey has dissolved completely and the syrup has slightly thickened, remove from the heat. Add the dried chamomile flowers and lemon peel, cover, and steep for 20 minutes. Strain solids, reserving the syrup. Cool completely before using. Store in the refrigerator for 1 week.

There's no better nightcap in my opinion than a hot toddy. The Chamomile Toddy is a slightly different variation on the classic, replacing whiskey with infused vodka, but it is delicious just the same.

2 oz pear-infused vodka (page 165)
4 oz hot chamomile tea
1 oz chamomile honey syrup
1/2 oz lemon juice
1/4 oz chamomile ginger pear shrub (page 157)

Combine hot chamomile tea, chamomile honey syrup, lemon juice, and shrub in a mug and stir lightly to combine. Add vodka and stir again. Enjoy warm.

Dandelion

Taraxacum officinale

There is no other flower that encapsulates the nostalgia of childhood more than the dandelion: finding one that has gone to seed, making a wish, and with pure joy, giving it a blow to set the seeds flying. Considered a weed and a nuisance, the dandelion gains its credibility due to its uses as medicine and food.

The dandelion's medicinal properties have been used in traditional Chinese medicine for over a thousand years. The dandelion roots and leaves were used as a restorative tonic for the bloodstream and a gentle diuretic for the digestive system. It's common to find dandelion tea and dandelion extract in modern apothecaries.

All parts of the dandelion are edible and delicious in salads, herbal wines, baking, and more. Rich in vitamins A, C, and E, and calcium, the young flowers are sweet like honey, the greens slightly bitter and crisp. The roots, when roasted, have a lovely nutty flavor.

FINE AND DANDY

makes 1 drink

Roasted dandelion root tea serves as a base for this winter warmer and adds a nutty richness to the drink. The warmth doesn't come only from the temperature of this drink, but it also appears in the heat of dried ancho chili peppers.

ROASTED DANDELION ROOT TEA

Sure, you can find dandelion root tea in the grocery store, but this recipe not only satisfies the DIY-er, but it gives you a reason to use and appreciate dandelions! Plus, I have to bet you've got some growing in your own yard. *Find the recipe on page 166.*

1 1/2 oz ancho chili-infused vodka (page 155)
1/2 oz creme de cacao
1/2 oz dry Curaçao
1/2 tsp tamarind paste
3 oz roasted dandelion root tea
3 drops of Amaro Sfumato Rabarbaro
smoking cinnamon

Light the end of a cinnamon stick and while it's smoking, hold under a heat-proof cocktail glass, allowing smoke to fill the glass. Set upright and pour dandelion root tea into the glass. Add the tamarind paste and stir. In a mixing glass, stir vodka, creme de cacao, dry Curaçao, and amaro until combined. Pour over the dandelion tea, giving it a stir to mix. Garnish with a dandelion and a smoking cinnamon stick.

Hibiscus

Hibiscus sabdariffa

When I close my eyes and imagine hibiscus flowers, I can practically hear the ocean, feel the sand between my toes and smell the salt in the air — possibly because my fondest memories of hibiscus flowers originate from my childhood in Florida, where hibiscus flowers dotted the pathways to the beaches.

Hibiscus flowers have many associations with historical folklore. A long-standing symbol of delicate and feminine beauty, the hibiscus worn behind the left ear promotes a woman as eligible; while worn behind the right ear, the bloom tells potential suitors that the woman is spoken for.

There are hundreds of species in the Hibiscus family, though *Hibiscus sabdariffa* is the most well known for its popular use in folklore and culinary applications. High in vitamin C as well as natural antioxidants, the calyx from these hibiscus flowers are often found in medicinal and flavorful teas.

SMOKY RITA

makes 1 drink

Meet Smoky Rita. She's Margarita's sultry older sister. She's spicy, a little sweet, and extra smoky. The addition of cardamom-flavored Agua de Jamaica adds the spice, and the combination of mezcal and palo santo adds the smoke.

AGUA DE JAMAICA

Agua de Jamaica literally translated means "Hibiscus Water". In this boosted version of the popular Mexican hibiscus tea, I like to add cardamom and orange slices for a little extra flavor. *Find the recipe on page 155.*

2 oz mezcal
1 oz triple sec
2 oz Agua de Jamaica (page 155)
1/2 oz lime juice
1/2 oz simple syrup
3–4 dashes of palo santo bitters
slice of lime
hibiscus peppercorn salt (page 162)
cinnamon stick

Rub rim of glass with lime, then roll into hibiscus peppercorn salt. Light a stick of cinnamon so that it begins smoking, and place it in the glass while preparing the drink. Combine mezcal, triple sec, Agua de Jamaica, lime juice, and bitters in a shaker over ice and shake until chilled. Remove the smoking cinnamon from the glass, add ice, and pour the drink.

Jasmine

Jasminum officinale

Jasmine, the night queen. A flower of seduction and mystery, evoking love and prophetic dreams. Ancient belief was that the sensuous aroma from jasmine penetrates the soul and opens up the emotions. Today it is often used to draw spiritual love or attract a soulmate.

There are nearly 200 species of jasmine native to South and Southeast Asia. The word *jasmine* is derived from the Arabic word *yasmin*, despite its not being originally native to Arabia. It means "fragrant flower." It is known for its intoxicating and sweet-smelling scent and is widely used as a fragrant ingredient in perfumes.

Jasmine-infused water is a traditional drink in Southeast Asia and can be traced back to the 17th century. Jasmine water has been used for centuries to add distinctive flavor to Thai rice, aka jasmine rice. The floral water not only adds a subtle sweetness but also a distinct floral aroma. It is important to note that only the species *Jasminum officinale* and *Jasminum sambac* are edible; all other Jasminum species or jasmine in other families are poisonous.

WHITE JASMINE SANGRIA

makes 12 servings

Who doesn't love a good sangria? This delicious white sangria is sweet, floral, tangy, and tart — ALL at the same time. It combines the sweetness of cantaloupe and the subtle floral flavor of jasmine with the tangy bite of ginger. It's perfect for a mild, spring day.

JASMINE GINGER GREEN TEA SIMPLE SYRUP

Jasmine green tea is one of the most well-known types of green tea in the world. It's subtly sweet and highly fragrant and gives a delightful addition to this drink. *Find the recipe on page 163.*

1 bottle of dry white wine
1 cup of triple sec
12-oz bottle of ginger ale
juice from 1 cantaloupe
1 cup jasmine ginger green tea syrup (page 163)
1/3 cup jasmine flower water
1 lime, sliced
4 kumquats, sliced

In a pitcher or glass serving container, combine wine, triple sec, ginger ale, cantaloupe juice, jasmine ginger green tea simple syrup, jasmine flower water, and fruit slices. Stir gently. Serve over ice. Garnish with fruit slices.

Orange Blossom

Citrus x aurantium

One whiff of an orange blossom's honey-kissed scent is enough to invoke memories of my childhood, playing amongst the citrus trees in my backyard. If you've ever been in the presence of a citrus tree in bloom, you're familiar with that fresh, ethereal scent of the flowers. It's calming, with the ability to ease stress and irritability.

The bitter orange tree is native to southern Vietnam and widely cultivated. The earliest mention of the sweet orange in Chinese literature dates from 314 BCE where it is said to have derived from a cross between pure mandarin and pomelo parents. It is thought to have been introduced into America by Spanish travelers. The bitter orange is used in orange flavored liqueurs such as triple sec, Grand Marnier, and Curaçao.

Orange blossoms, when distilled for their essential oil, leave behind the most gloriously aromatic by-product well-known in the cocktail industry: orange blossom water. It is a key ingredient in orgeat and many classic cocktails, but also finds its way into many delicious desserts and baked goods.

CREAMSICLE PUNCH

makes 16 drinks

In 1763, Benjamin Franklin wrote a letter to James Bowdoin, a friend with whom he corresponded about mutual scientific interests for nearly 40 years. In that letter he included a recipe for Milk Punch that would become popular in the cocktail industry for years to come. Milk Punch is based on science, using acids to curdle the milk, removing tannins. The process was used by bartenders for preserving drinks in the days before refrigeration, but the crystal clear, silky result is stunning. Stripped of the acidity and tannins, Creamsicle Punch is lightly floral and silky smooth.

2 cups VSOP cognac
2 cups aged rum
peels of 2 lemons
peels of 2 oranges
1 cinnamon stick
2 star anise
5 cardamom pods
1 cup lemon juice
1 cup orange juice
1 cup orange blossom water
1 cup water
2 cups sugar
2 cups whole milk

Find the full recipe and instructions on page 158.

Red Clover

Trifolium pratense

I can remember spending hours kneeling on my front lawn, pawing through the clovers, hunting for a four-leafed one. And how special it felt to finally find one! Some say that on average, there are 10,000 three-leaf clovers for every four-leaf clover. As such, legend has it that if one finds a four-leaf clover, it will bring the finder good fortune and protection.

Red clover is one of about 250 species of the Trifolium family. The word *trifolium* comes from Latin meaning "three leaves." It is native to Western Asia and parts of Europe, though it can be found growing wild on most every continent. It is particularly fond of thickets but grows easily in fields or along roadsides.

Red clover's flowers and leaves are edible and can be added to salads, tea, soups, baked goods, syrups, and jellies. In addition to its edibility, traditional Chinese doctors used it as a tonic for colds, and at one time the Chinese burned it as incense. Native Americans used it as a salve for burns.

CLOVERJITO

makes 1 drink

Cloverjito combines two of my favorite summer drinks, iced tea and the classic rum-based Mojito, into a fresh cocktail.

CLOVER SUN TEA

2 tbsp red clover blossoms
1 tbsp dried mint
1 tbsp dried lemon balm
1 tsp dried lemon peel
cold water

Add all the clover flowers and herbs to a 64-oz jar, and top with water. Allow to infuse in warm sunlight for 4 hours. Strain into a clean jar and store in the refrigerator for 1 week.

2 oz white rum
2 oz clover sun tea
2 limes, cut into wedges
handful of fresh mint leaves
2 tsp sugar
sparkling water

In the bottom of the glass, muddle the mint leaves, lime wedges, and sugar together to release their juices. Fill the glass with ice. Pour over the rum and clover sun tea. Stir with a straw to combine. Garnish with a red clover flower and mint leaves.

Glam Garnishes

Garnishing adds a unique style or a taste element to a cocktail. Sometimes a cocktail isn't a cocktail without the proper garnish. A slice of lime. A lemon peel. Candied ginger. Bourbon cherries. An edible flower. The garnish completes the cocktail experience. Edible flowers not only make an easy cocktail garnish, but, in my opinion, they can make the simplest cocktail downright glamorous. Flowers add a bright burst of color and often a subtle floral aroma that's perfect for many drinks.

Aster

Aster spp.

Asters make up about 180 species of tiny, star-like flowers in the Asteraceae family. The name *aster* comes from the Greek word *aster* meaning "star," which refers to the shape of their flower heads. Additionally, the name can be traced back to Greek mythology where it was believed that the Greek goddess Astraea was so saddened with the lack of brightness in the sky that she began to cry. From her tears, asters began to bloom. She decided to name them *asters,* referencing the stars she wished to see in the sky.

The aster symbolizes many different things. The Farmer's Almanac suggests that asters were primarily known as symbols of powerful love. Perhaps inspired by this symbolism, the aster has been named as the flower for the 20th wedding anniversary. Furthermore, it was thought that the perfume from the burning leaves of asters could drive away evil serpents.

The aster is used as a medicinal herb in Chinese medicine to treat a variety of ailments, from hangovers to digestive problems. The flowers can be eaten fresh or dried for a multitude of uses.

BRANDY DAISY

makes 1 drink

The Brandy Daisy is a member of a group of daisy cocktails. Daisy cocktails first gained popularity in the late 19th century. Multiple variants have developed over the years, including the use of other base spirits, such as whiskey or gin. Brandy is my favorite for this version, but feel free to swap out another base spirit for a different experience!

HONEY ROSE SYRUP

A honey syrup adds richness and more mouth feel than a simple syrup. *Recipe on page 162.*

2 oz brandy
1 barspoon gold rum
1 barspoon maraschino liqueur
1/2 oz honey rose syrup (page 162)
1/2 oz lemon juice
soda

Add the brandy, rum, rose hip liqueur, honey rose syrup, and lemon juice to a shaker with ice, and shake until chilled. Strain into a chilled glass. Top with soda and stir gently. Garnish with a cluster of asters.

Cosmos

Cosmos bipinnatus

It is said that 16th-century Spanish explorers discovered cosmo flowers growing wild on the hillsides in Mexico and brought them back with them to Madrid. They were mesmerized by the flower's petals, which are quite symmetrical, arranged in opposite pairs. They gave them the name *cosmos* to symbolize their order and harmony with the rest of the universe.

Cosmos are one of my favorite flowers to grow in the garden. They don't require too much attention and easily reseed, sprouting up more plants each year. Their bright and cheerful petals make lovely cut flowers and exceptional additions to salads and cocktails.

DUSK IN THE COSMOS

makes 1 drink

The exact origin of the Cosmopolitan cocktail is unclear, but, like me, many have Sex and the City to thank for introducing them to this flirty drink. The Cosmo was a hit in the late 90s, and when served in a martini glass, it feels fancy and sophisticated but it was easier to consume than a traditional martini.

A classic Cosmopolitan lists cranberry juice as one of the ingredients, which is most often sold in sweetened form unless it states "100% juice." Either one works in this drink, but using the latter allows you to customize the sweetness to your taste. If you find Dusk in the Cosmos to be too tart, feel free to add more cranberry simple syrup to taste.

2 oz dragonfruit & lemon peel infused vodka (page 159)
1/2 oz Cointreau
1/2 oz lime juice
1/4 oz unsweetened cranberry juice
1/4 oz cranberry simple syrup (page 158)
a pinch of edible glitter
orange peel twist

Add the dragonfruit & lemon peel infused vodka, Cointreau, lime juice, cranberry juice, cranberry simple syrup, and edible glitter to a shaker and shake over ice until chilled. Strain into a chilled glass. Rim a martini glass with the orange peel twist, gently expressing the oils along the rim, and garnish with a cosmo flower.

Freesia

Freesia x hybrida

The freesia flower conveys friendship and innocence, which symbolizes how it was given its name. It was first described as a genus in 1866 by Christian Friedrich Ecklon, who was researching plants in South Africa. He then named the flower after his friend and fellow botanist, Friedrich Freese. This gained freesia the distinction of being the ultimate flower of trust in *The Language of Flowers*.

Today there are over 1,400 different cultivars of freesia, ranging in color from red, orange, and yellow, to purple, pink, and white. Due to their delicate fragrance, freesias are one of the most popular cut flowers in the wedding industry. The scent of freesias is said to enhance mood and reduce stress levels.

The scent of freesias can be very sweet, like summer fruits, or citrusy and peppery, with a sharp zing. Their popular fragrance is used in aromatherapy and perfumery. The blossoms add a rich scent to syrups, salads, and sorbets and work flawlessly as a cocktail garnish. Be sure to only consume the petals as the sap can cause skin irritation.

FOUR FIFTY-SIX

makes 1 drink

Four Fifty-Six is so close to that magical hour. It's practically five o'clock and quite acceptable to start making a cocktail. Four Fifty-Six is a riff on the classic Gimlet. It's a perfect drink to get the evening started.

COCONUT WATER SYRUP

Using coconut water in place of water in a simple syrup adds a velvety richness. *Find the recipe on page 157.*

2 1/2 oz gin
1/2 oz coconut water syrup (page 157)
1/2 oz lime juice
freesia flowers
lime wheel

Combine gin, coconut water syrup, and lime juice in a cocktail shaker with ice and shake until chilled. Strain into a chilled glass. Lightly press the petal of a freesia flower around the rim and discard. Garnish with a fresh freesia flower and lime wheel.

Fuchsia

Fuchsia spp.

Fuchsia flowers are a very popular flower for the home garden due to their striking colors. Their bright blooms are a favorite to hummingbirds, providing them with sweet nectar. Though they're native to Central and South America, there are now more than 100 different species of fuchsia growing throughout the world.

Many will associate the vibrant pink color with fuchsia. But fuchsia gives the color its name, not the other way around. It was discovered over 300 years ago by Charles Plumier, a French monk and botanist, on the island of Hispaniola. He then named it in honor of German botanist Leonhart Fuchs, who was the first botanist to compile a botanical glossary.

Most people do not realize that this common hanging basket flower, is edible and quite delicious. Fuchsia blossoms are crunchy and tangy with a slight tart-sweet flavor and are lovely in a salad or frozen into ice cubes. They also produce edible fruits. It is said that the berries from *Fuchsia splendens* are the best-tasting of all the species, with the flavor reminiscent of citrus and pepper.

PINK PALINDROME

makes 1 drink

Pink Palindrome is about as bright and pink as it gets, but don't let the color fool you. Its sultry and unexpected smoke flavors are topped with the strong aromatic mist from absinthe.

DRAGONFRUIT-INFUSED PISCO

Place a piece of frozen dragonfruit in a jar with pisco, and allow it to thaw completely. Strain the pisco through a mesh filter and discard the solids.

1 1/2 oz dragonfruit-infused pisco
1/2 oz lemon juice
1 oz burnt sugar syrup (page 156)
3 dashes of yarrow bitters (page 149)
absinthe mist

In a shaker, combine the dragonfruit-infused pisco, lemon juice, and burnt sugar syrup, and shake vigorously for 10 seconds or until the outside of the shaker is frosty. Pour into a glass filled with ice. Dash with bitters and mist with absinthe. Garnish with a fuchsia blossom.

Gladiolus

Gladiolus spp.

Gladioli were some of my mom's favorite flowers. We always had a big, dramatic bouquet of them displayed in a vase behind our grand piano. She would place the flowers, usually in bright colors of red or orange, into a vase, then sit down to play at the piano.

Gladioli are impressive in stature with their long, pointed shape. Their name comes from the Latin word *gladius*, which means "sword" and symbolizes strength and pride. Therefore, it's only natural that gladioli were associated with gladiators. It has been said that Roman gladiators wore gladiolus around their necks during battles to help them win and to protect them from death.

The genus Gladiolus contains about 300 species, mostly native to South Africa, where the flowers and corms were used for centuries as medicine and food. Crushed gladiolus flowers would soothe a blister or scratch. The flowers have a taste similar to lettuce and can be stuffed or used in salads. Sweet nectar can be sucked from the flower, but only the petals should be eaten. Discard the anther and the middle of the blossoms before consuming.

VIKING SWORD

makes 1 drink

Aquavit is a Nordic spirit, primarily distilled in Scandinavia. It gets its distinct flavor from the herbs and spices that it is distilled with, two of which are caraway and dill. Viking Sword has additional Nordic flavor from lingonberry jam.

LINGONBERRY JAM

Lingonberries are small, red berries that are the Scandinavian equivalent of North American cranberries. They're mostly wild-foraged, but you can find lingonberry jam online or in specialty grocery stores.

1 1/2 oz gin
1/2 oz aquavit
3/4 oz lime juice
2 tsp lingonberry jam
soda water
1 bar spoon of overproof rum
a pinch of cinnamon
lemon twist

Add the lingonberry jam into the bottom of a glass, and top with ice. Shake the aquavit, gin, and lime juice in a shaker with ice until chilled. Pour into prepared glass and fill with soda water. Top with overproof rum and cinnamon. Garnish with a gladiolus bloom and lemon twist.

Hollyhock

Alcea rosea

It was believed that fairies inhabited the blooms of hollyhock flowers. Victorian children told stories of fairies using the blossoms as skirts and called the seed pods "fairy cheese" due to their resemblance to a wheel of cheese. There is even a recipe dating from the 1600s which includes hollyhock in the ingredients that would allow mortals to see the fairy folk.

The ancient Egyptians made wreaths of hollyhock to be buried with mummies. Many believe this indicated that hollyhocks served as an important connection with the circle of life in Egyptian culture, leading the dead into the afterlife.

Indeed, hollyhocks have had many uses over time. The flower's leaves are moisturizing, so they were often added to baths or conditioning soaps. Violet-colored hollyhock flowers have been used to make a pale periwinkle blue dye. Hollyhock flowers have almost no flavor of their own but are a lovely addition sprinkled over desserts or garnishing a cocktail.

PLUM MULLED WINE

makes 1 drink

Mulled wine is one of my absolute favorite drinks for any chilly night. I love allowing it to gently mull on the stove top for a few hours, making the house smell of warm spices. In this extra boozy version, I added the plums and homemade plum brandy to provide more depth and flavor.

PLUM BRANDY

Plum Brandy or Slivovitz is a fruit brandy made from plums all over Central and Eastern Europe. It is quite simple and rewarding to make on your own at home. I find it tastes best with Italian plums, but any type of plum will work. *Find the recipe on page 165.*

1 750 mL bottle of red wine
1 cup of plum brandy (page 165)
1 cup of ruby port
1/4 cup brown sugar
1 orange, sliced
10 Italian plums
5 star anise
4 cinnamon sticks
12 cloves

Combine the wine, brandy, port, brown sugar, orange, plums, star anise, cinnamon sticks, and cloves in a saucepan. Bring to a gentle simmer over low heat for 30 mins and up to 1 hour. Do not boil. Strain to remove solids and serve warm, garnished with a hollyhock.

Orchid

Orchidaceae family

You may know of the orchid as being a quintessential tiki garnish, but there is a whole lot more to orchids than that. For example, did you know that the vanilla bean comes from the world's only fruit-bearing orchid? Or did you know that the family Orchidaceae is very large, consisting of approximately 28,000 species, distributed in about 763 genera? Or that orchids may have originated over 85 million years ago? Indeed there is a lot to know about orchids.

Ancient Greeks believed that consuming orchid tubers could increase fertility and traditional Chinese medicine made use of different types of orchids to help with indigestion, headaches, and eyesight. Orchid extract is even used in skincare to reduce the appearance of fine lines.

Orchid flowers are the most common floral garnish in the food and drink industry. The orchid is often referred to as the workhorse of garnishes, making any drink more pleasing. The petals are described as having a crisp, peppery flavor that is similar to endive or nasturtium. Most orchids are considered safe to eat, however some species can irritate the stomach. When choosing orchids, be sure you're purchasing ones that are specifically marked as food grade.

THE ORCHID

makes 1 drink

The Orchid is a riff on the Mai Tai; it swaps white rum with tequila and mezcal for something tropical and earthy.

ORCHID ICE CUBES

Place one small orchid into an ice cube tray. Cover with distilled water and freeze until solid. Keep frozen until ready to use.

**Sauvie Shrubs is my favorite online source for fresh shrubs, but if you would like to try making your own, follow the recipe for Concord Grape Shrub on page 157, swapping the ingredients.*

1 oz blanco tequila
1/2 oz mezcal
3/4 orange Curaçao
*1/2 oz Sauvie Shrubs Papaya Lime Coconut shrub**
1/4 oz lime juice
1/2 orgeat
1/4 oz dark rum

Add orchid cubes to a chilled glass and set aside. Shake tequila, mezcal, Curaçao, shrub, lime juice, and orgeat over ice until chilled. Strain into prepared glass and top with a dark rum float. Garnish with an orchid flower.

Snapdragon

Antirrhinum majus

Tell me — do you have memories of squeezing the sides of a snapdragon to open and close the dragon's mouth? Snapdragons were some of my favorite flowers as a child, and I remember doing that anytime I'd see one! In Greek, the word *anti* means "like," while *rhinum* means "snout," which refers to the appearance of the flowers in the genus Antirrhinum. And something even more fascinating about snapdragons comes when they go to seed; the shape of the seed pods resembles a little skull!

The common snapdragon is native to rocky areas of Europe, the United States, and North Africa. They are easily grown and make beautiful cut flowers. In fact, snapdragons were considered one of the top five cut flowers grown in North America in the 1950s.

Although some cultivars have an almost candy-like scent, snapdragons are rather bland in flavor, usually making it on an edible flower list for their ornamental value, rather than for taste. However, if you're one to believe in legends, one states that snapdragons are able to restore youthfulness and beauty to any woman who eats them.

MADAME BUTTERFLY

makes 1 drink

I wanted to create a drink that tastes the way the flower smells. Madame Butterfly combines the bitterness of Suze, a gentian liqueur, with the flavor from the mint lime syrup, resulting in a candy-like and complex drink.

MINT LIME SIMPLE SYRUP

Mint and lime zest are one of my favorite combinations. The zest from the lime has a lightly floral undertone, and when paired with mint, it takes on a candy-like flavor. *Find the recipe on page 163.*

3/4 oz blanco tequila
3/4 oz Suze
1/4 oz yellow Chartreuse
3/4 oz pineapple juice
1/2 oz mint lime simple syrup (page 163)
white port rinse

Pour a small amount of white port into a chilled glass, swirl it to coat the glass, and discard. Combine the blanco tequila, Suze, yellow Chartreuse, pineapple juice, and mint lime simple syrup together in a shaker over ice and shake until chilled. Strain into the prepared glass and garnish with a snapdragon flower.

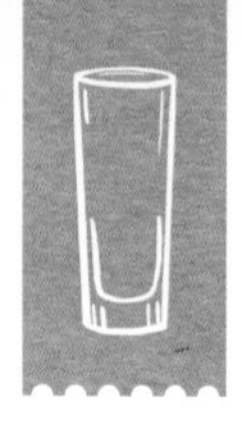

Squash Blossom

Cucurbita pepo

Squash blossom flowers are a generic name for any flower from a summer or winter squash. They are the edible flowers of the squash plant and usually come in colors of yellow and orange. The flowers have a subtle flavor similar to zucchini and can be eaten raw, but they're best when stuffed with cheese and fried. The female flowers are the part of the plant that produce a fruit. The male flowers don't produce any fruit, so you never had to feel bad about picking them for frying!

VERDE MARY

makes 1 drink

If you've ever had fried squash blossoms, you know how delicious they are. So simple, light, and crisp, and in my opinion, quite possibly the best garnish to top the Verde Mary with.

FRIED SQUASH BLOSSOMS

12 zucchini blossoms
1 cup all-purpose flour
12 oz pilsner beer
4 oz herbed goat cheese
sea salt
vegetable oil, for frying

Heat about 2 inches of oil over medium heat until a deep-fry thermometer reads 350°. Stuff the blossoms with herbed goat cheese. Combine flour and salt in a medium bowl, then whisk in beer until almost smooth. Dip blossoms one at a time into the batter. Gently lay them in the oil and cook the blossoms until golden brown (about 2-3 minutes), flipping once. Transfer to paper towels to drain. Sprinkle with sea salt and enjoy while warm.

The Verde Mary is my green, flower-infused take on a Bloody Mary. Originating in the early 20s, the Bloody Mary has earned a place on brunch menus, reputable to cure hangovers. The cocktail has become known for its glam garnishes: celery, olives, pickles, citrus wedges, charcuterie, bacon, shrimp, and more. This variation uses straight-from-the-garden ingredients for the infused vodka and the tomatillo juice.

2 oz Verde Mary infused vodka (page 168)
4 oz Verde Mary juice (page 169)
1/2 teaspoon Worcestershire sauce
1 tsp pepperoncini juice
1 pinch cumin
1 tsp smoked paprika
2 tbsp sea salt

Mix paprika and salt together in a bowl. Rim glass with lime wedge and dip into the paprika salt. Add remaining ingredients to a shaker and shake over ice for 10 seconds. Pour into prepared glass and pile on the garnishes!

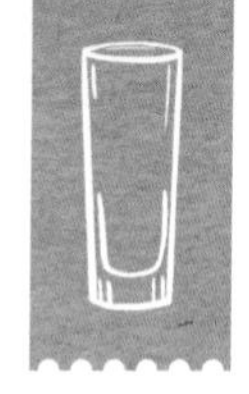

Sweet Alyssum

Lobularia maritima

Sweet alyssum is a ground cover flower native to the Mediterranean, with tiny clustered blossoms that range from white and light pink to lilac and deep violet. Sweet alyssum is a member of the family Brassicaceae, which comprises broccoli and mustard. Though the blossoms have a faint scent of honey, its edible leaves taste somewhat like a broccoli leaf and are often added to salads for spice and flavor.

Alyssum, though edible, is most commonly used in the garden. Sometimes called "carpet flowers," alyssum is planted among rock structures to add a pop of color spilling out onto an otherwise plain landscape.

The name *alyssum* comes from the Greek word *lyssa* meaning "madness" and the "a" means "against," giving alyssum its meaning today, "without madness." It was said that alyssum's pleasant honey-like aroma promoted peaceful energy. Furthermore, in the language of flowers, sweet alyssum means "worth beyond beauty."

PABLO'S DAUGHTER

makes 1 drink

Pablo's Daughter is a fresh take on the Paloma, a classic and bubbly grapefruit/tequila cocktail. With the additions of mandarin, lime, rosemary, and Campari, then garnished with a bright, purple alyssum flower for a pop of color, it's a cocktail fit for the child of an artist.

GRAPEFRUIT ROSEMARY SIMPLE SYRUP

Grapefruit makes the base flavor for this cocktail, bringing in sweet citrus notes. When combined with rosemary, it adds a wonderfully unexpected herbal punch. *Find the recipe on page 161.*

2 oz blanco tequila
1 oz grapefruit juice
1 oz mandarin juice
1/2 oz lime juice
1/2 oz grapefruit rosemary simple syrup (page 161)
1/4 oz Campari
grapefruit bubbly water
grapefruit slice
mandarin slice

Add tequila, grapefruit juice, mandarin juice, lime juice, simple syrup, and Campari to a shaker and shake over ice until chilled. Strain into a glass over ice and top with bubbly water. Garnish with sliced grapefruit, mandarin, and a stem of alyssum.

Marvelous Mocktails

Mocktails have come a long way over the years, emerging as something fab and delicious. What was once forgotten in a mixologist's drink list is now something that must not be overlooked. This has been aided by the increase of spirit-free producers over the past few years. Alcohol-free options have moved away from the old familiars like Virgin Daiquiris, Shirley Temples, or flavored sodas. Whether you're abstaining from alcohol completely or just want a booze-free evening, there are plenty of fun mocktail options to try.

Bee Balm

Monarda didyma

Bee balm, otherwise known as wild bergamot or oswego tea, is native to North America. The genus was named for the Spanish botanist Nicolás Monardes, who wrote a book in 1574 describing plants of the New World.

Bee balm has long been used by Native Americans as a medicinal herb. It was used as a natural antiseptic, as well as to aid digestion, to calm nerves, and even to soothe bee stings. A symbol of wealth and prosperity, it is believed to be useful for attracting money if you carry a few sprigs in your wallet.

Bee balm also has a history in the kitchen. It is related to the mint family and has a spicy herbal flavor similar to oregano. The cheerful flowers resemble fireworks in bright colors of red, purple, and pink. The fresh flowers yield a beautiful pink color when steeped into tea or vinegar and are great for spicing up beverages.

BEE ROSY

makes 1 drink

BEE BALM MINT SIMPLE SYRUP

1 cup cold water
1 cup sugar
1/2 cup bee balm petals
3 springs of mint

Gently remove the bee balm petals from the stem, and place them into a jar with the mint. Pour cold water over the petals and steep in the refrigerator for 4 hrs or overnight. Strain the petals and mint leaves and add the sugar. Shake until the sugar is dissolved. Store in the refrigerator for up to 1 week.

Bee Rosy is an thirst-quenching mocktail with a little bit of spice. It's refreshing on its own, or add 1 oz of Cocchi Americano if you're wanting a low-proof cocktail.

2 oz watermelon-rose agua fresca (page 169)
1 oz bee balm mint syrup
1/2 oz lime juice
1/2 oz lemon juice
soda water
2 slices of jalapeño

Muddle two jalapeño slices in the bottom of a cocktail shaker with the citrus juices. Add watermelon agua fresca and bee balm mint syrup, and shake over ice until chilled. Strain into a glass with ice and top with soda water.

Dahlia

Dahlia spp.

The history of the dahlia dates back to ancient Aztec Empire. The Aztecs grew hundreds of varieties of dahlias and used them for food, medicinal, and agricultural purposes. The hollow stems of dahlias were used to construct aqueducts to aid in their irrigation system. The tubers were grown as a food crop and today the sweet potato-shaped dahlia tubers are still considered a staple ingredient in Oaxacan cuisine.

The dahlia symbolizes kindness and grace. One of the most popular and sought-after Dahlia cultivars in recent years is a gorgeous, dinner plate-sized Cafe au Lait. Ranging in color from a blush pink/peach to a creamy beige, Cafe au Laits have grown very popular in the wedding industry for their pastel billowy blooms.

CAFÉ AU LAIT

makes 2 drinks

Café au Lait is a drink of strong brewed coffee, to which steamed milk is added. Since I realize most people do not have a coffeehouse-grade steamer at home, I'm using a frother to achieve a similar effect. My version includes the addition of hazelnut orgeat and extra orange blossom water for a special treat.

DAHLIA BLOSSOM SUGAR

1 tbsp dried orange peels
1 tbsp dried dahlia petals
1 tsp ground cardamom
4 tbsp sugar
1 tbsp red sugar sprinkles

In a spice grinder, combine orange peels, dahlia petals, and cardamom and pulse until finely ground. Add to sugar and sprinkles. Use within 1 month.

16 oz brewed coffee
12 oz whole milk
2 oz orange blossom water
1 oz hazelnut orgeat (page 161)
dahlia blossom sugar

Divide the orange blossom water and hazelnut orgeat into two mugs. Whisk to combine. Pour the brewed coffee over the orgeat equally into each mug. Stir to combine.
Gently warm the milk in a pan over medium heat until it begins to bubble on top. Pour the warm milk into a heat-proof jar and submerge the tip of the frother just below the surface of the milk. Froth the milk until a fluffy foam forms. Gently pour the milk into the coffee, swirling as you pour, ending with the foam. Sprinkle with dahlia blossom sugar.

Honeysuckle

Lonicera spp.

Sweet, sweet nectar of the honeysuckle! I'm sure you, like me, have a memory of plucking a honeysuckle blossom from a bush and sucking the nectar from the base of the flowers. In my mind, it is truly one of nature's delights!

The sweet folklore behind honeysuckle centers around love and happiness. It is believed that honeysuckle brought into the home will help ensure happy days and a good marriage for the people who live there. Additionally, the scent of honeysuckle is said to clear the mind, sharpen intuition, encourage psychic dreams, and sweeten any mood.

A tea can be made from the heavily perfumed blossoms. It is important to note that among the 180 species of honeysuckle, not all are edible. Additionally, even if the flowers are edible, the leaves and fruits of some species are *very toxic*. The flowers from *Lonicera japonica* and *Lonicera periclymenum* are generally considered safe.

HONEYSUCKLE LIMEADE

makes 32 servings

Honeysuckle Limeade is quite possibly one of my very favorite summer drinks. It's simple, refreshing, and easy to put together for a crowd. I love having a non-alcoholic batch made in the refrigerator so my kids can pour some anytime they come in from playing outside. *Try making it into a cocktail by adding 1 1/2 oz of toasted coconut-infused vodka, page 168.*

HONEYSUCKLE SIMPLE SYRUP

Honeysuckle simple syrup is the perfect way to capture the flavor and scent of the honeysuckle blossoms. *Find the recipe on page 162.*

1 1/2 cups lime juice
12 cups cold water
1 cup honeysuckle syrup (page 162)
1/4 cup toasted coconut simple syrup (page 168)
8 Thai basil leaves

Lightly muddle the Thai basil leaves with the lime juice in the bottom of a pitcher. Pour all ingredients into the pitcher and stir to combine. Store limeade in the refrigerator and use within 1 week. To serve, pour over ice and garnish with a lime wheel and honeysuckle blossom.

Sage

Salvia officinalis

Salvia is a large genus of plants with nearly 1000 species. There are several widely used species in the genus, including white sage, pineapple sage, clary sage, culinary sage, and rosemary. Sage has been listed as one of the essential herbs in culinary preparations due to its unique, savory flavor.

The name *Salvia* comes from the Latin word *salvere* meaning "to heal" or "to save." Sage has been used as a medicinal herb since ancient times. It was said that eating sage daily would give one immortality. It was used in everything from hair care and teeth cleaning to healing insect bites, reducing fevers, and calming mental conditions. In the garden, it was believed to determine prosperity; less sage meant a failing business, while more sage meant the business would thrive.

The flower colors differ between species, ranging from pale pink and violet to bright red and deep blue. They have a strong sage flavor and are wonderful infused into oil or honey, or chopped and mixed with sea salt.

SPARKLING SAGE PUNCH

makes 24 servings

What's a party without punch? In this non-alcoholic punch, flavors swirl together delightfully. Feel free to swap in your favorite spirited dry vermouth or dry white wine if you're looking for a little more kick in your punch. Perfect for year-round get togethers.

SAGE-FLOWER SIMPLE SYRUP

Sage-flower simple syrup is the sweet and savory, and a perfect addition to this punch. *Find the recipe on page 167.*

2 750-mL bottles sparkling apple cider
2 cups non-alcoholic dry vermouth
2 cups soda water
1/2 cup sage-flower simple syrup (page 167)
1/4 cup apple butter
1/4 cup lemon juice
2 apples, sliced and seeds removed
6 cinnamon sticks
5 sprigs sage flowers

Pour all ingredients into a punch bowl and give it a light stir to mix. Top with fresh sage flowers.

Rose

Rosa spp.

It is believed that currently there are around 30,000 varieties of roses worldwide. The *Old Farmer's Almanac* states that the oldest rose still around today, *Rosa gallica var. officinalis*, was in existence over 4,000 years ago. It is known as "Apothecary's Rose," because of its use by herbalists for both skin and mind benefits. The natural oils from rose petals help lock moisture into dry skin, while the scent of roses is said to ease anxiety and comfort the mind.

Considering that roses are one of the oldest and most adored flowers, it's easy to see why they've gained a permanent space in many societies. Ancient Greeks associated the rose with the goddess of love, Aphrodite, who is often seen with roses adorning her head, feet, or neck. Newly married couples in ancient Rome chose to be crowned with roses and rose petals, and paintings of roses were discovered in many ancient Egyptian tombs.

Rose buds, petals, and hips are all edible. The flavor of roses ranges from flavorless to bitter, sour to sweet, slightly spicy to herbal, and even appley to minty. The most popular edible species are *Rosa rugosa alba, Rosa rugosa, Rosa damascena,* and *Rosa gallica*.

SECRET GARDEN

makes 1 drink

What I love most about the Secret Garden is how much it feels like a cocktail in its presentation. It's built in the same way as a classic sour cocktail with egg-white foam, but is completely booze-free.

CARDAMOM ROSE SIMPLE SYRUP

Cardamom is one of my favorite culinary spices. When mixed with rose, it becomes a sultry and sweet combination. *Find the recipe on page 156.*

2 oz iced rose hip tea
1 oz lemon juice
1/2 oz cardamom rose simple syrup (page 156)
egg white
5 dashes of Peychaud's bitters
rose water mist

Dry-shake the egg white vigorously for 30 seconds. Add rose hip tea, lemon juice, cardamom rose simple syrup, and a handful of ice to the shaker, and shake for 30 seconds more. Strain into a chilled glass and mist with rose water.

Resources

This is a list of my favorite companies from which you can purchase things you need for making flower-infused cocktails.

EDIBLE FLOWERS

Gourmet Sweet Botanicals

Fresh edible flowers and micro greens.

Mountain Rose Herbs

Dried flowers, herbs, spices.

Baker Creek

Heirloom seeds to grow your own edible flowers.

GLASSWARE & TOOLS

Barfly

An extensive collection of mixology tools.

Etsy

One of my favorite resources for vintage drinkware.

Viski

Premium glassware.

SPIRITS, MIXERS, & MORE

I have many favorite brands of spirits and mixers. A few of my very favorites, many of which are mentioned in this book, are: The Botanist, Elijah Craig, KOVAL, Espolòn, Empress 1908, Crater Lake Spirits, St. George Spirits, Wild Roots Spirits, Clear Creek Distillery, Lyre's Spirits, Sauvie Shrubs, Meadowland Syrups, Floral Elixirs, Yes Cocktail Co., Som Cordials, Liber & Co, BG Reynolds, PDX ICE, Scrappy's Bitters, The Bitter Housewife, Fever Tree, and Broadus Bees. There are many more which can be found on my website at www.theflowerinfusedcocktail.com.

SAFETY

Plants for a Future, www.pfaf.org

Expanded information on over 7,000 different species, including edibility, medicinal uses and contradictions, hardiness zones, habitat, hazards, and more.

RECIPES

This is a collection of additional recipes used throughout the book. They're called for in specific drinks, but feel free to be creative, have fun, and experiment with mixing them into new libations!

AGUA DE JAMAICA

6 cups water
1 cup dried hibiscus flowers
1/2 cup sugar
1 tbsp decorticated cardamom
1 cinnamon stick
2 star anise
1 orange, sliced

Bring 2 cups of water to a boil. Add the hibiscus flowers and continue to simmer for 10 minutes. Turn off the heat and add the sugar, cardamom, cinnamon, star anise, and orange slices. Cool completely. Strain into a pitcher and add remaining water. Stir to combine. Use within 1 week.

ANCHO CHILI-INFUSED VODKA

Add 1 dried ancho chili pepper to a jar and cover with vodka. Give it a good shake daily for 2 days. Strain and store in the refrigerator for up to 1 week.

APRICOT CARDAMOM SHRUB

5 apricots, pitted and chopped
1 tsp cardamom pods
1 orange peel
1/2 cup sugar
1/2 cup apple cider vinegar

Place the apricots, cardamom pods, and orange peel into a jar, and cover with sugar. Place in the refrigerator overnight. Strain the liquids through a cheesecloth into a clean jar. Push lightly on the apricots to release all the juices. Add vinegar to the jar and place in the refrigerator until the sugar dissolves. Use within 1 week.

BASIL FLOWER INFUSED DRY VERMOUTH

To infuse the vermouth, add 6 or 7 basil flowers to a jar and cover with vermouth. Give them a good shake daily for 2 days. Strain and store in the refrigerator for up to 1 week.

BASIL FLOWER SYRUP

1 cup sugar
1 cup water
10 basil flowers

Combine sugar and water in a small pot and bring to a gentle simmer over medium heat. Once the sugar has dissolved completely and the syrup has thickened, remove from the heat. Add the basil flowers, cover, and steep for 10 minutes. Strain syrup through a fine mesh strainer and cool completely. Store in the refrigerator for 1 week.

BITTERSWEET SALT

1/4 cup sugar
1/4 cup salt
1 dried orange peel

In a spice grinder, pulse the orange peel until ground into a fine powder. Combine with sugar and salt in a jar, cover tightly, and shake until combined. Store in a dry place for up to 1 month.

BORAGE SIMPLE SYRUP

1 cup sugar
1 cup water
1/2 cup borage blossoms

Gently remove the borage blossoms from the stem. Combine sugar and water in a small pot and bring to a gentle simmer over medium heat. Once the sugar has dissolved completely and the syrup has thickened, remove from the heat. Add the borage blossoms, cover, and steep for 20 minutes. Cool completely before using. Use within 1 week.

BROWN BUTTER WASHED RUM

12 oz gold rum
1/2 cup butter

Pour the rum into a heat-proof jar. Melt butter in a pan over medium-high heat until it begins to brown and become fragrant. Allow it to cool slightly, then pour into the jar with the rum. Give it a good swirl and then bring to room temperature. Once it has cooled to room temperature, place the jar in the freezer overnight. Remove the jar from the freezer and, using a knife, poke a hole in the layer of butter and strain the infused rum through a coffee filter into a clean jar. Store in the refrigerator.

BURNT SUGAR SIMPLE SYRUP

1 cup sugar
1 cups water

Slightly burn the sugar in a small pot over medium-low heat, being careful that it does not melt or stick to the bottom of the pan. When it begins to brown, add water and bring to a gentle simmer over medium heat. Once the sugar has dissolved completely, remove from heat. Strain out any chunks that may have formed. Cool before using. Store in the refrigerator for 1 week.

CANDIED KUMQUATS

12 kumquats, sliced into thin rounds
1 cup sugar
1/2 cup water

In a saucepan, bring the sugar and water to a simmer over medium heat. Once the sugar has dissolved completely, remove from heat. Add the kumquats to the pot and soak for 1 hour.
Drain the kumquat pieces, reserving the syrup. Place the syrup-coated kumquats on a parchment-paper lined baking sheet and bake at 175 F for 1 hour. Flip the kumquats and bake for another 10 minutes. Cool completely before storing. Keep in a dry place for up to 1 month.

CARDAMOM ROSE SIMPLE SYRUP

1/4 cup dried rose petals
1 tbsp cardamom pods
1 cup sugar
1 cup water
a splash of rose water

Combine sugar and water in a small pot and bring to a gentle simmer over medium heat. Once simmering, add the cardamom and simmer for 1 minute more. Remove from the heat and add the rose petals. Cover and steep for 30 minutes. Strain syrup through a fine mesh strainer and cool completely. Add a splash of rose water and pour into a clean bottle. Store in the refrigerator for 1 week.

CHIVE BLOSSOM SALINE

2 dried chive blossoms
1 tbsp salt
3 oz water

Combine the salt and water together in a jar and shake until clear. Add the dried chive blossoms and shake again, then strain. Transfer to a dropper dispenser.

CHAMOMILE GINGER PEAR SHRUB

4 ripe pears, chopped
1 1/2 cups sugar
1-inch knob of ginger, chopped
1/4 cup chamomile flowers
1 1/2 cups apple cider vinegar

Place the chopped pears in a glass jar and top with the sugar. Toss them lightly to evenly coat them with sugar. Add the chopped ginger and chamomile and shake again. Cover the mixture and place in the refrigerator for 48 hours. Strain the pears, squeezing them to achieve as much liquid as possible. Pour in the apple cider vinegar and stir to combine. Place the mixture back in the refrigerator for up to 5 days before using. Keep refrigerated for up to 6 months.

CHERRY BLOSSOM TEA

Commercially produced cherry blossom tea is available, but make sure the tea uses cherry blossoms, not artificial flavors, and be sure to dust off the extra salt. It's used to preserve the blossoms but can make your cocktail unnecessarily salty!

1/2 cup cherry blossoms
8 oz water
3 drops of ume plum vinegar

Remove the calyx and wash the flowers gently. Bring the water to a gentle boil, then remove from the heat. Add the cherry blossoms and allow to steep for 5 minutes. Add the ume vinegar and chill before using.

CINNAMON-INFUSED TEQUILA

Place 2 cinnamon sticks into a jar with tequila and give it a good shake. Remove cinnamon sticks after 3 days and store the tequila in a dry place.

COCONUT OIL WASHED GIN

12 oz gin
4 tbsp coconut oil

Melt the coconut oil in a heat-proof jar in the microwave for 30 seconds or until fully melted. Allow to cool slightly, then add the gin to the jar. Give it a swirl and bring to room temperature. Once it has cooled to room temperature, place the jar in the freezer overnight. Remove the jar from the freezer, poke a hole in the layer of coconut oil, and strain the gin through into a clean jar. Store in the refrigerator and use within 1 week.

COCONUT WATER SIMPLE SYRUP

1 cup sugar
1 cup coconut water

Combine sugar and coconut water in a jar and shake until the sugar dissolves. Store in the refrigerator and use within 1 week.

CONCORD GRAPE SHRUB

1 pound of Concord grapes, deseeded
1 tbsp dried cornflower petals
1 tsp cloves
1/2 cup sugar
1/2 cup apple cider vinegar

Place grapes in a saucepan over medium heat. Mash and squeeze them slightly to release some juices. Continue to heat until the grapes are cooked through.
Remove from heat and stir in the cornflower petals, cloves, sugar, and vinegar. Cover and steep overnight at room temperature. Strain in a jar. Store in the refrigerator and use within 1 week.

CRANBERRY SIMPLE SYRUP

1 cup sugar
1 cup water
1/2 cup fresh cranberries

Combine sugar and cranberries in a small pot and bring to a gentle simmer over medium heat. Gently mash the cranberries, encouraging them to release their juices. Once the sugar has dissolved completely, add the water and bring to a gentle simmer. Once the syrup has thickened, remove from the heat and steep for 30 minutes. Strain the syrup into a clean jar, removing the cranberries. Cool completely before using. Use within 1 week.

CRÈME DE MÛRE AU BASILIC

Crème de Mûre or blackberry liqueur, is incredibly simple to make at home. My version adds basil, which offsets the sweetness with an herbal touch.

5 cups blackberries
1/2 cup Thai basil flowers and leaves
1 bottle medium-bodied red wine
1 1/2 cups sugar
1/2 cup vodka

In a large jar, combine the blackberries, basil, and red wine, slightly muddling the berries and basil. Cover and infuse for 2 days in the refrigerator. Strain through cheesecloth to remove the solids. Pour the wine and berry mixture into a saucepan and add the sugar. Bring to a gentle simmer and stir until the sugar is dissolved. Continue to simmer for 5 minutes. Remove from heat and allow to cool before stirring in the vodka. Pour into a clean jar. Store in the refrigerator for up to 1 year.

CREAMSICLE PUNCH

2 cups VSOP cognac
2 cups aged rum
peels of 2 lemons
peels of 2 oranges
1 cinnamon stick
2 star anise
5 cardamom pods
1 cup lemon juice
1 cup orange juice
1 cup orange blossom water
1 cup water
2 cups sugar
2 cups of whole milk

Add the citrus peels, cinnamon stick, star anise, and cardamom pods to a large jar and cover with cognac and rum. Cover and infuse for 24 hours.
Discard the solids. Add all of the ingredients except for the milk to the infused alcohol and stir to combine.
Add the whole milk to a separate jar. Slowly and gently pour the cocktail mixture into the milk, and stir to combine. Cover with a lid and allow to rest on the counter for 2 hours. Transfer to the refrigerator and allow the mixture to infuse for 24 hours.
Using a coffee filter, strain the liquid into a clean jar, using the ring of the lid or a rubber band to keep the filter in place. Resist the temptation to touch or press the curds, and allow it to drip through on it's own. It will take a long time, but it is worth it. Repeat the filtering process until the cocktail is crystal clear. Store in the refrigerator.

DRAGONFRUIT & LEMON PEEL INFUSED VODKA

1 lemon, peeled
6 oz vodka
1 oz frozen dragonfruit

Add vodka and lemon peels to a jar and keep in the refrigerator for up to a week. Add dragon fruit to the jar with vodka and allow it to thaw completely. Strain the vodka through a mesh filter and discard the solids.

ELDERFLOWER LIQUEUR

1 1/2 cups vodka
10 cups of elderflower blossoms
1/2 cup sugar
1/2 cup water
1 inch piece of lemon peel

Remove the elderflower blossoms from stems completely and allow them to wilt slightly. Add 4 cups of blossoms to the vodka, making sure that they're fully submerged in the liquid. Cover and refrigerate overnight.
Using a fine mesh strainer, strain the flowers from the vodka. Add 4 more cups of flowers to the vodka, and return to the fridge and allow to infuse again overnight. Pour the elderflower-infused vodka through a coffee filter to strain out any leftover debris.
Over medium-low heat, cook the sugar, water, and remaining 2 cups of blossoms with the lemon peel until combined, about 5 minutes. Remove from heat and cool. Once the syrup has cooled, strain the solids. Then combine the elderflower syrup and elderflower-infused vodka in a sealable glass bottle and shake. For best flavor, allow the liqueur to rest for a minimum of 12 hours. Store at room temperature or in the refrigerator for up to 6 months.

ELDERFLOWER SIMPLE SYRUP

1 cup elderflower blossoms
1/2 cup sugar
1/2 cup water
1-inch piece of lemon peel

Gently remove the blossoms from the stems. Combine sugar and water in a small pot and bring to a gentle simmer over medium heat. Once the sugar has dissolved completely and the syrup has thickened, remove from the heat. Add the elderflower blossoms and lemon peel, cover, and steep for 30 minutes. Cool completely before using. Store in the refrigerator and use within 1 week.

ELECTRIC MANDARIN CORDIAL

2 cups water
2 cups sugar
12 buzz buttons
3 mandarins, sliced thin
zest from 1 lemon

Bring water and sugar to a boil in a saucepan and then remove from heat. Stir to fully dissolve the sugar. Add the buzz buttons, lemon zest, mandarin slices, and juice to the sugar and water syrup. Cover and infuse overnight. Pour the mixture through a fine mesh strainer and bottle. Keep refrigerated for up to 3 months

FIG-INFUSED RYE

To infuse the rye, add 6 or 7 dried figs to a jar and cover with rye. Give them a good shake daily for 5 days. Strain and store in the refrigerator for up to 1 week. Reserve the figs for garnishing. They are also quite tasty!

FALERNUM SYRUP

1/3 cup blanched almonds
1 tbsp cloves
3-inch piece of ginger, chopped
3 medium limes, zested and juiced
1 cup water
1 1/2 cup sugar

In an oven preheated to 200 degrees, toast almonds, cloves, and ginger until fragrant, about 5 minutes. Combine sugar and water in a small pot and bring to a gentle simmer over medium heat. Once the sugar has dissolved completely, remove from the heat. Add the almonds, cloves, ginger, lime zest, and lime juice. Cover and leave to steep overnight. Strain using a nut milk bag to retain all the syrup. Store in the refrigerator for 1 week.

FIR-INFUSED VODKA

12 oz vodka
5 branches of Douglas fir, needles stripped and lightly chopped.
1 branch with needles intact

Submerge the fir needles in vodka and store in a dark place. Shake daily and allow to infuse for at least 7 days. Strain into a clean jar and store in the refrigerator for up to 3 weeks.

FORSYTHIA HONEY LIQUEUR

1 1/2 cups vodka
10 cups forsythia blossoms, divided
2/3 cup honey
1/2 cup water
1 inch piece of orange peel, pith removed
3 cloves
1 cinnamon stick

Remove the forsythia blossoms from the stem and give them a good shake to remove any bugs or debris. Allow them to wilt slightly, coaxing out their sweet fragrance. Add 4 cups of blossoms to the vodka, making sure that they're fully submerged in the liquid. Cover and refrigerate overnight.

Using a fine-mesh strainer, strain the flowers from the vodka. Add 4 more cups of flowers to the vodka and return to the fridge and allow to infuse again overnight. Pour the forsythia-infused vodka through cheesecloth or a coffee filter to strain out any leftover debris.

Over medium-low heat, cook the honey, water, orange peel, clove, and cinnamon until it is combined, about 5 minutes. Add the remaining 2 cups of forsythia flowers and steep for 5 minutes. Cool completely.

Once the syrup has cooled, remove the solids, reserving the infused honey. Then combine the forsythia-infused honey syrup and forsythia-infused vodka in a sealable glass bottle and shake. For best flavor, allow the liqueur to rest for a minimum of 12 hours. Store at room temperature or in the refrigerator for up to 6 months.

FRESH GREEN JUICE

Any combination of your favorite green fruits and vegetables can be used here, but my favorites are green apple, spinach, celery, lime, and pineapple. Together, they work really well in any cocktail. If you don't have a juicer, you can blend them together with a little water and strain through a cheesecloth.

GINGER MINT SIMPLE SYRUP

1 cup sugar
1 cup water
1-inch piece of ginger, chopped
1 sprig of mint

Combine sugar and water in a small pot and bring to a gentle simmer over medium heat. Once the sugar has dissolved completely and the syrup has thickened, remove from the heat. Add the ginger and mint, cover, and steep for 30 minutes. Cool completely before using. Use within 1 week.

GRAPEFRUIT ROSEMARY SIMPLE SYRUP

1 cup sugar
1 cup water
1/2 grapefruit, sliced, with peels removed
1 sprig of rosemary

Combine sugar and water in a small pot and bring to a gentle simmer over medium heat. Once the sugar has dissolved completely, add the grapefruit and stir for 1 minute, lightly mashing the fruit. Remove from the heat. Add the rosemary, cover and steep for 30 minutes. Cool completely before using. Use within 1 week.

HAWTHORN ROSE CORDIAL

2 cups water
2 cups sugar
2 tbsp dried hawthorn berries
3 tbsp dried rose petals
1 tbsp dried rose hips
1 cinnamon stick
1 mandarin, sliced thin
zest from 1 lemon

Bring water and sugar to a boil in a saucepan and then remove from heat. Stir to fully dissolve the sugar. Add the hawthorn berries, rose petals, rose hips, cinnamon stick, mandarin slices, and lemon zest to the sugar and water syrup. Cover and infuse overnight. Pour the mixture through a fine mesh strainer and bottle. Keep refrigerated for up to 1 month.

HAZELNUT ORGEAT

2 cups chopped hazelnuts
1 1/2 cups sugar
1 1/4 cups water
1 tsp orange zest
1/2 tsp orange blossom water

Pulse hazelnuts in a food processor until finely ground. Combine the sugar and water in a pot over medium heat and stir until sugar dissolves completely. Boil the syrup for 3 minutes, then add in the ground hazelnuts and orange zest. Turn the heat down to low and simmer for another 3 minutes, then slowly increase the temperature to medium-high. Just before it starts to boil, remove it from the heat and cover with a lid.

Allow the covered nut mixture to infuse for at least 3 hours or up to 8 hours. Then, strain it through 2 layers of cheesecloth, discarding the solids. Stir the orange flower water into the nutty syrup. Use a small funnel to portion the orgeat into bottles or a jar. Store in refrigerator for up to 2 weeks.

HIBISCUS PINK PEPPERCORN SALT

1 tbsp dried hibiscus
1 tsp pink peppercorns
1/4 cup salt

With a mortar and pestle, grind hibiscus and pink peppercorn until finely ground. Combine with salt in a jar, cover tightly, and shake until combined. Store in a dry place for up to 1 month.

HONEY ROSE SIMPLE SYRUP

1/2 cup orange blossom honey
1/2 cup water
3 tbsp dried rose petals

Bring water to a gentle simmer over medium heat. Once simmering, add the honey and rose petals and stir until the honey has dissolved into the water. Remove from the heat and steep for 30 minutes. Strain the rose petals and cool completely before using. Store in the refrigerator and use within 1 week.

HONEYSUCKLE SIMPLE SYRUP

1 cup honeysuckle blossoms
1/2 cup sugar
1/2 cup water

Gently remove the blossoms from the stems. Combine sugar and water in a small pot and bring to a gentle simmer over medium heat. Once the sugar has dissolved completely and the syrup has thickened, remove from the heat. Add the honeysuckle blossoms, cover, and steep for 30 minutes. Cool completely before using. Store in the refrigerator and use within 1 week.

HOPPED BOURBON CHERRIES

4 cups sweet cherries, pitted
1/2 cup water
1/2 cup sugar
1 split vanilla bean
1 cinnamon stick
1 strip orange peel
1 tbsp dried hop flowers
1 cup bourbon

Divide cherries into jars. Whisk together the water, sugar, and vanilla bean over medium heat until combined. Reduce heat to low and stir in the cinnamon, orange peel, and hops. Cover and allow mixture to simmer for 15 minutes. Remove from heat, and strain out the solids. Add the bourbon and allow the mixture to cool slightly before pouring over cherries. Can be kept in the refrigerator for up to 3 months.

IPA SIMPLE SYRUP

1/2 cup of your favorite citrus-forward IPA (my favorite is Boneyard RPM)
1/2 cup water
1 cup sugar
1/4 cup dried hop flowers

Combine the IPA, water, and sugar in a small pot and bring to a gentle simmer over medium heat. Once the sugar has dissolved completely and the syrup has slightly thickened, remove from the heat. Add the dried hop flowers, cover, and steep for 20 minutes. Strain solids, reserving the syrup. Cool completely before using. Store in the refrigerator for 1 week.

JASMINE GREEN TEA SIMPLE SYRUP

1 cup sugar
1 cup water
2 tbsp loose jasmine green tea
1-inch piece of ginger, chopped

Bring water to a gentle simmer over medium heat. Remove from the heat and add the loose jasmine tea. Steep for 3 minutes and strain, reserving the liquid. Add the sugar and bring back to a simmer. Once the sugar has dissolved completely and the syrup has thickened, remove from the heat. Add the ginger, cover, and steep for 30 minutes. Cool completely before using. Store in the refrigerator and use within 1 week.

KUMQUAT SIMPLE SYRUP

1 cup sugar
1 cup water
10 kumquats

Combine sugar and water in a small pot and bring to a gentle simmer over medium heat. Once the sugar has dissolved completely and the syrup has thickened, remove from the heat. Add the kumquats, gently mashing them with a muddler. Cover and steep for 30 minutes. Cool completely before using. Store in the refrigerator and use within 1 week.

LAVENDER INFUSED GIN

To infuse the gin, add 1 tbsp fresh lavender to a jar and cover with gin. Give it a good shake and place in the refrigerator overnight. Strain and store in the refrigerator for up to 1 week.

LAVENDER EARL GREY SIMPLE SYRUP

1 cup sugar
1 cup water
2 tbsp loose earl Grey tea
1 tbsp dried lavender

Bring water to a gentle simmer over medium heat. Remove from the heat and add the loose earl Grey tea and dried lavender. Steep for 3 minutes and strain, reserving the liquid. Add the sugar and bring back to a simmer. Once the sugar has dissolved completely, remove from the heat. Cool completely before using. Store in the refrigerator and use within 1 week.

MARSHMALLOW SIMPLE SYRUP

1 cup sugar
1 cup water
5 jumbo marshmallows, chopped

Combine sugar, water, and marshmallows in a small pot and bring to a gentle simmer over medium heat. Once the sugar has dissolved completely and the syrup has thickened, remove from the heat. Cool completely before using. Store in the refrigerator and use within 1 week.

MINT LIME SIMPLE SYRUP

1 cup sugar
1 cup water
1 lime, sliced
1 sprig of mint

Combine sugar and water in a small pot and bring to a gentle simmer. Once the sugar has dissolved completely and the syrup has thickened, remove from the heat. Add the sliced limes and mint. Cover and steep for 30 minutes. Cool completely. Store in the refrigerator and use within 1 week.

MEXICAN HOT COCOA

2 cups of milk of your choice
2 wedges of Taza 70% Cacao Puro
1 tsp vanilla extract
1 tsp ancho chili powder
1 cinnamon stick
sugar to taste

Place all the ingredients in a large pot, over medium-low heat. Whisk until the chocolate wedges begin to melt. Increase the heat and continue whisking until the chocolate begins to form a foam on the top. Keep warm.

ORANGE SEA SALT CORDIAL

2 cups water
2 cups sugar
3 oranges, sliced thin
1 tbsp key lime juice
zest from 1 orange
1/2 tsp sea salt

Bring water and sugar to a boil in a saucepan and then remove from heat. Add the orange slices, key lime juice, orange zest, and sea salt to the syrup. Cover and infuse overnight. Strain through a fine mesh strainer. Keep refrigerated for up to 1 month.

ORANGE VANILLA SHRUB

1 naval orange, sliced
1 split vanilla bean
1/2 cup sugar
1/2 cup champagne vinegar

Place the sliced orange and vanilla bean in a glass jar and top with the sugar. Toss them lightly to evenly coat them with sugar. Cover the mixture and place in the refrigerator for 48 hours. Strain the oranges, squeezing them to achieve as much liquid as possible. Pour in the vinegar and stir to combine. Place the mixture back in the refrigerator for 5 days. Strain completely into a new jar. Keep refrigerated for up to 6 months.

OSMANTHUS SWEET VERMOUTH

1 bottle pinot grigio
4 gm wormwood
1 3/4 gm sarsaparilla
1/2 gm osmanthus flowers
1/2 gm hibiscus flowers
1/2 gm chamomile flowers
1/2 gm gentian root
1/2 gm angelica root
1/2 gm orange peel
1/4 gm lemon verbena
1/4 gm cinnamon chips
1/4 gm dandelion root
1/8 gm holy basil
1/8 gm wild cherry bark
1/3 vanilla bean, chopped
1 cup brandy
1 cup manzanilla sherry
1 cup sugar
1/4 cup water

Combine all of the herbs and spices with 1 cup of pinot grigio and bring to a boil. Remove from the heat and add the remaining pinot grigio and manzanilla sherry. Place in the refrigerator to infuse for at least 5 hours. Strain into a clean jar. Lightly combine sugar and water together in a saucepan. Heat on medium until it begins to bubble. Resist the urge to stir it too much, allowing the sugar to caramelize. Once caramelized, add the brandy by stirring very gently. Remove from heat.

Pour the infused wine mixture into the brandy mixture, and stir to combine. Pour into clean bottles and store in the refrigerator for up to 1 month.

PANSY SUGAR CUBES

1 cup superfine sugar
2 tsp Angostura bitters
5 dried pansy flowers
2 tsp water

In a coffee grinder, pulse the dried pansy flowers until they're powdery. Combine sugar, bitters, pansy powder, and water in a bowl. Mix until well combined, similar to the texture of wet sand. Pack the mixture into a mini square silicone mold, pressing down on each square so that they're packed tight. Let mixture sit out to dry overnight. When sugar has hardened, pop cubes out of the molds. If you don't have a silicone mold, you can spread the mixture out in a bread pan, pressing down hard, and cut the cubes to size. Store in an airtight container for up to 1 month.

PASSION FRUIT SIMPLE SYRUP

1/2 cup sugar
1/2 cup water
1/4 cup passion fruit purée

Combine sugar and water in a small pot and bring to a gentle simmer over medium heat. Once the sugar has dissolved completely and the syrup has thickened, remove from the heat. Add the passion fruit purée and stir until combined, Cool completely before using. Store in the refrigerator and use within 1 week.

PEAR-INFUSED VODKA

Peel and core 1 pear and place in a jar. Cover completely with vodka and lightly mash the pear. Place in the refrigerator overnight. Strain and store in the refrigerator for up to 1 week.

PINEAPPLE WEED SIMPLE SYRUP

1 cup pineapple weed flowers, plucked from the stem
1/2 cup sugar
1/2 cup water

Combine sugar and water in a small pot and bring to a gentle simmer over medium heat. Once the sugar has dissolved completely and the syrup has thickened, remove from the heat. Add the pineapple weed flowers, cover, and steep for 30 minutes. Strain and cool completely before using. Store in the refrigerator and use within 1 week.

PLUM BRANDY

2 lbs Italian plums, pitted and sliced
1 cup sugar
1 cinnamon stick
1 strip lemon peel
1/2 vanilla bean
2 cups vodka
1/2 cup brandy

In a large 32-oz jar, mix the plum pieces with the sugar, making sure that all the slices are coated. Add the cinnamon stick, lemon peel, vanilla bean, vodka, and brandy, and shake to combine.
Ferment at room temperature for 2 weeks, turning the jar over each day to aid in dissolving the sugar. Once the sugar has dissolved, transfer the jar to a cool, dark cabinet and allow to continue fermenting for 3 months.
After 2 months, strain the solids and pour into clean bottles.

PUFFED AMARANTH

4 tbsp amaranth seeds
1 cup sugar
1 cup water

Preheat a high pot over medium-high heat. Be sure to test that the pan is hot enough by adding a few amaranth seeds to the pot. If they pop immediately, it's ready. Working 1 tbsp at a time, spread amaranth on the bottom of the pot. Shake the pot to be sure that all the seeds pop and don't burn. Once the popping stops, pour puffed amaranth into a bowl and repeat.

PUFFED AMARANTH SIMPLE SYRUP

1/2 cup puffed amaranth
1 cup sugar
1 cup water

Combine sugar and water in a small pot and bring to a gentle simmer over medium heat. Once the sugar has dissolved completely and the syrup has thickened, remove from the heat. Add the puffed amaranth, cover, and steep for 10 minutes. Strain syrup through a fine mesh strainer and cool completely before using. Store in the refrigerator for 1 week.

RHUBARB SIMPLE SYRUP

1 cup sugar
1 cup water
3 stalks rhubarb, chopped

Combine sugar, water, and rhubarb in a small pot and bring to a gentle simmer over medium heat. Allow the syrup to simmer until the rhubarb begins to break down, about 3 minutes. Remove from the heat, cover, and steep for 10 minutes. Strain syrup through a fine mesh strainer and cool completely before using. Store in the refrigerator for 1 week.

ROASTED DANDELION ROOT TEA

1 tbsp roasted dandelion root
8 oz water

To roast the dandelion root, place it on a baking sheet in a single layer and roast at 350°F for 15 minutes, stirring halfway through.

To make the tea, bring water to a boil in a small pot. Add the roasted dandelion root and boil for 5-10 minutes. Strain the root pieces with a fine mesh strainer.

SAFFRON SUGAR CUBES

1 cup superfine sugar
2 tsp orange bitters
a pinch of saffron threads
2 tsp water

Using a mortar and pestle, grind the saffron threads until they're powdery. Combine sugar, bitters, saffron powder, and water in a bowl. Mix until well combined, similar to the texture of wet sand. Pack the mixture into a mini square silicone mold, pressing down on each square so that they're packed tight. Let mixture sit out to dry overnight. When sugar has hardened, pop cubes out of the molds. If you don't have a silicone mold, you can spread the mixture out in a bread pan, pressing down hard, and cut the cubes to size. Store in an airtight container for up to 1 month.

SAGE FLOWER SIMPLE SYRUP

1 cup sugar
1 cup water
5 sage flower sprigs

Combine sugar and water in a small pot and bring to a gentle simmer over medium heat. Once the sugar has dissolved completely and the syrup has thickened, remove from the heat. Add the sage flowers, cover, and steep for 15 minutes. Strain and cool completely before using. Store in the refrigerator and use within 1 week.

SAGE SIMPLE SYRUP

1 cup sugar
1 cup water
10 sage leaves

Combine sugar and water in a small pot and bring to a gentle simmer over medium heat. Once the sugar has dissolved completely and the syrup has thickened, remove from the heat. Add the sage leaves, cover, and steep for 30 minutes. Strain and cool completely before using. Store in the refrigerator and use within 1 week.

SCHISANDRA SIMPLE SYRUP

1 cup sugar
1 cup water
1 tbsp dried schisandra berries

Combine sugar and water in a small pot and bring to a gentle simmer over medium heat. Once the sugar has dissolved completely and the syrup has thickened, remove from the heat. Add the schisandra berries, cover, and steep for 30 minutes. Strain and cool completely before using. Store in the refrigerator and use within 1 week.

SPICED CALENDULA SIMPLE SYRUP

1 cup sugar
1 cup water
1 tsp cloves
1 tsp allspice berries
1 cinnamon stick
1/4 cup dried calendula petals

Combine the sugar and water in a small pot and bring to a gentle simmer over medium heat. Once the sugar has dissolved completely and the syrup has slightly thickened, remove from the heat. Add the spices, cover, and steep for 20 minutes. Add the calendula petals in the last 5 minutes of steeping. Strain solids, reserving the syrup. Cool completely before using. Store in the refrigerator for 1 week.

STRAWBERRY PEONY PINK PEPPERCORN CORDIAL

2 cups water
2 cups sugar
2 cups peony petals, allowed to wilt*
1 tbsp lemon juice
1 orange, sliced thin
1 cup of strawberries, quartered

Bring water and sugar to a boil in a saucepan and then remove from heat. Stir to fully dissolve the sugar. Add the peony petals, citric acid, lemon juice, orange slices, and strawberries into the sugar and water syrup. Cover and infuse overnight. Pour the mixture through a fine mesh strainer and bottle. Keep refrigerated for up to 3 months.

*Store-bought peonies will not work for this, as most have been sprayed or treated. Grow your own or purchase the most fragrant peonies from a local grower you know and trust. Dried rose petals make a wonderful substitution in a pinch.

SUGAR SNAP PEA SIMPLE SYRUP

1 cup sugar
1 cup water
5 sugar snap peas, sliced in half

Combine sugar and water in a small pot and bring to a gentle simmer over medium heat. Once the sugar has dissolved completely and the syrup has thickened, remove from the heat. Add the sugar snap peas, cover and steep for 30 minutes. Strain and cool completely before using. Store in the refrigerator and use within 1 week.

SUNFLOWER ORGEAT

2 cups toasted sunflower seeds
1 1/2 cups sugar
1 1/4 cups water
1/2 tsp orange blossom water

Pulse sunflower seeds in a food processor until finely ground. Combine the sugar and water in a pot over medium heat and stir until sugar dissolves completely. Boil the syrup for 3 minutes, then add in the ground sunflower seeds. Turn the heat down to low and simmer for another 3 minutes, then slowly increase the temperature to medium-high. Just before it starts to boil, remove it from the heat and cover with a lid.

Allow the covered nut mixture to infuse for at least 3 hours or up to 8 hours. Then, strain it through 2 layers of cheesecloth, discarding the ground sunflower seeds. Stir the orange flower water into the nutty syrup. Use a small funnel to portion the orgeat into bottles or a jar. Store in refrigerator for up to 2 weeks.

TOASTED COCONUT SIMPLE SYRUP

1/4 cup coconut flakes
1 cup sugar
1 cup water

To toast the coconut flakes, heat them on a warm pan over medium heat, stirring constantly until browned.

Combine sugar and water in a small pot and bring to a gentle simmer over medium heat. Once the sugar has dissolved completely and the syrup has thickened, remove from the heat. Add the toasted coconut, cover, and steep for 10 minutes. Strain syrup through a fine mesh strainer and cool completely before using. Store in the refrigerator for 1 week.

TOASTED COCONUT INFUSED VODKA

Toast coconut in the same method as the above recipe. Cover completely with vodka. Place in the refrigerator overnight. Strain and store in the refrigerator for up to 1 week.

VERDE MARY INFUSED VODKA

To infuse the vodka, start by filling a large jar with your favorite green garden ingredients such as green tomatoes, celery, cucumbers, and peppers. Then add other classic Bloody Mary ingredients like garlic, lemons, dill, and carrots. Fill to the top with your favorite vodka. Refrigerate for 5 days. Like it hot? Add in a whole serrano pepper on the last day of infusing. Strain vodka into a clean jar and store in the refrigerator.

VERDE MARY JUICE

3 medium tomatillos, chopped
1/2 cucumber, peeled and chopped
2 stalks of celery, chopped
1 green apple, peeled and chopped
1 serrano pepper
1/2 poblano pepper
1/2 green bell pepper
3 sprigs of cilantro
juice from 1 lime
juice from 1 orange
1/4 cup water

Add all ingredients to a blender and purée until very smooth. Run juice through a fine mesh strainer to filter. Refrigerate up to one week.

WATERMELON ROSE AGUA FRESCA

1 cup sugar
1 cup water
10 sage leaves

Combine sugar and water in a small pot and bring to a gentle simmer over medium heat. Once the sugar has dissolved completely and the syrup has thickened, remove from the heat. Add the sage leaves, cover, and steep for 30 minutes. Strain and cool completely before using. Store in the refrigerator and use within 1 week.

WILD ROSE BITTERS

4 oz 100 proof vodka
dried wild rose petals
2 tbsp chopped gentian
1/2 tsp sarsaparilla

Place the dried rose petals, gentian, and sarsaparilla into an 8-oz jar. Pour the vodka into the jar, just so that it covers the top of the botanicals. Cover the jar and store it in a cool, dark place for at least 1 week. Shake the jar when you think about it, every other day if possible. After 1 week, strain and reserve the liquid.
If you prefer to sweeten your bitters, you can add 1 oz of simple syrup at this point. Store in a dark bottle for up to 1 year.

YARROW SIMPLE SYRUP

1 cup sugar
1 cup water
1/2 cup fresh yarrow blossoms

Combine sugar and water in a small pot and bring to a gentle simmer over medium heat. Once the sugar has dissolved completely and the syrup has thickened, remove from the heat. Add the yarrow blossoms, cover, and steep for 20 minutes. Strain and cool completely before using. Store in the refrigerator for 1 week.

This book is a love letter to flowers and an ode to the appreciation of blooms beyond the vase. It is a result of an amazing team of cheerleaders, supporting my process along each step of the way.

This book would not be what it is without my adoring and encouraging friends: Laurel, Ash, Jade, Jess, Angelina, Mandy, Angi, Terie, Julie, Jen, and many more — it's with your continual support that I wrote and finished this book. Your participation in the journey molded this book into what it is today.

To my children: Wolf, you sparked my love of flowers. Your deep love for them inspired me to expand my knowledge of them. And Orin, thank you coining "mocktail time" in our house and for always being up for tasting anything I made for you — spirit-free of course.

To my editors, Camille, Kate, and Lotsie: a million thank you's for keeping my it's/its and quotation marks in line.

To my parents, Sherilynn and Ben: Thank you for teaching me to follow my dreams and to not give up easily. Thank you for being my guiding light and allowing me to shine my creativity.

And lastly, to my loving husband, Levi: Thank you for always being my honest critic when I was developing new cocktails. Having you by my side while I stirred drinks and chatted on and on about flower folklore encouraged and motivated me to produce this book. I'm endlessly grateful for your love and support of my flower-infused lifestyle.

And with that...

Cheers!

About the Author

ALYSON BROWN IS A FLOWER ENTHUSIAST & COCKTAIL CREATOR.

Alyson founded her business, Wild Folk Flower Apothecary, in 2017 as a way to share her love of flowers with the world. Flowers became her life. She went on to work with the Central Oregon Wildflower Show to collect and identify wildflowers, host workshops weaving intentions of flowers into botanical creations, plan a flower-infused Solstice dinner in her backyard, design many flower crowns, and mix many flower-infused cocktails.

Though she currently calls the high deserts of Central Oregon her home, she often refers to her southern roots and love for the beach, having grown up just minutes from the Gulf Coast beaches in Florida. She lives in Bend, Oregon, with her husband, two young boys, a black cat, and a fluffy dog. When she's not mixing flower-infused cocktails, she runs a creative services business in which she specializes in brand photography and graphic design, and in her spare time she enjoys hiking, paddleboarding, and gardening.

Index

Page numbers in **bold** indicate where a picture of a flower shown; page numbers in *italics* indicate where a flower is used as an ingredient in a recipe.

T

V

W